Asset Protection: A Guide For Professionals

Howard Rosen Esq.
Patricia A. Donlevy-Rosen Esq.

Coral Gables, Florida
ProtectYou.com

Copyright © 2014 Howard Rosen Esq. and Patricia A. Donlevy-Rosen Esq.
All rights reserved.

ISBN: 1501078623
ISBN 13: 9781501078620
Library of Congress Control Number: 2014916112
CreateSpace Independent Publishing Platform
North Charleston, South Carolina

TABLE OF CONTENTS

I. INTRODUCTION · 1
   A. Definition of Asset Protection Planning · · · · · · · · · · · · · · · 2
   B. Traditional Asset Protection Methods and Their
      Inherent Problems · 3
      1. Outright Gifts · 3
      2. Gifts in Trust—General · 3
      3. Co-Ownership of Property—aka Concurrent Estates · · · 4
         a. Tenancies by the entireties. · · · · · · · · · · · · · · · · · · · 4
         b. Joint tenancy with right of
            survivorship (JTWROS). · 5
         c. Tenants in common. · 6
      4. Other · 6

II. LIMITED PARTNERSHIPS · 9
   A. Asset Protection Aspects · 9
      1. Charging Order Concept · 10
         a. Background and history. · 10
         b. Definition. · 11
         c. Effect of charging order. · 11
         d. Summary. · 12
      2. What Does the Internal Revenue Service Say about
         Charging Orders? · 12

B. US Tax Consequences of Creation and Use of
   Limited Partnerships 13
   1. Income Tax 13
      a. Creation of limited partnership. 13
      b. Ongoing use of limited partnership. 14
   2. Estate/Gift Tax 15

III. LIMITED LIABILITY COMPANIES 17
   A. Background 17
   B. Asset Protection Aspects 18
   C. US Tax Consequences of Creation and Use of
      Limited Liability Companies 18
      1. Income Tax 18
         a. Treatment as a partnership: 19
         b. Treatment as a corporation: 19
         c. Treatment as a disregarded entity: 19
      2. Estate/Gift Tax 20

IV. TRUSTS 21
      1. Retained Powers/Controls. 22
      2. Self-Settled Spendthrift Trust. 22
      3. Creditor Accessibility Rule
         (aka "maximum potential interest rule"). 23
   A. Trusts in Non-Community Property Jurisdictions .. 23
      1. Asset Protection Aspects 23
         a. Domestic trusts 24
            i. Working definition. 24
            ii. Discussion. 24
            iii. State asset protection trust laws. .. 29

Table Of Contents

   b. Offshore (Foreign Situs) Trusts · · · · · · · · · · · · · · 31
    i. Working definition. · 31
    ii. Discussion. · 32
    iii. Selecting the APT jurisdiction. · · · · · · · · · · · · 33
  2. US Tax Consequences · 49
   a. Domestic (US) trusts. · 49
   b. Offshore trusts. · 49
    i. Classification issues. · 49
    ii. US income tax Consequences of Creation. · · · · · 52
    iii. US income tax Consequences— Operation. · · · 52
    iv. US estate/gift/GST tax Consequences. · · · · · · · · 53
B. Trusts for Settlors Owning Community Property —
Special Considerations[108] · 55
C. Protective Trust Provisions · 57
 1. Discretionary Distribution Provision · · · · · · · · · · · · · 57
  a. Description. · 57
  b. Effect. · 58
 2. Spendthrift Provision · 59
  a. Description. · 59
  b. Effect. · 62
 3. Duress Provision · 62
  a. Background/description. · 62
  b. Effect. · 64
 4. Flight Provision · 65
  a. Description. · 65
  b. Effect. · 67
 5. Trust Protector Provision · 68
  a. Description. · 68
  b. Effect · 70

      6. Other Protective Provisions ············· 72
         a. Extension provision. ················ 72
         b. Principal and income allocation provision. ······· 72
         c. Revision of beneficial interests. ············ 73
         d. Custodian trustee provision. ············ 73
  D. Offshore Asset Protection Strategies. ············ 74
     1. Cash and Publicly Traded Securities (liquid assets) ··· 75
     2. Immovable Assets: Real Estate, Equipment,
        LLC Member Interests, Etc. ················ 76
     3. Entity Trusts ····················· 77
     4. Combination Structures ··············· 78
     5. Group Trusts ···················· 79
     6. Enhanced IRA Protection ·············· 80
  E. What Should a Personal Asset Protection Trust
     Include at a Minimum? ·················· 81

V. FRAUDULENT TRANSFERS/CONVEYANCES—
   VOIDABLE TRANSACTIONS ················ 82
  A. General ······················· 84
     1. Definition ····················· 84
        a. The transfer. ·················· 86
        b. Which creditors are protected?. ············ 88
     2. Determination of Intent — "Badges of Fraud" ······ 91
     3. Effect of a Court Finding a Fraudulent Transfer ···· 93
  B. Special Transfer Considerations ············ 93
     1. 18 U.S.C. § 1032: Fraud on the RTC or FDIC ········ 93
     2. Bankruptcy Issues ················· 96
     3. Other Special Considerations············· 98

Table Of Contents

VI. **EXEMPTION PLANNING—STATE LAW PROVIDED ASSET PROTECTION** · 100
   A. Homestead Exemption · 100
   B. Wage Account Exemptions · 101
   C. Annuity Exemptions · 102
   D. Qualified Retirement Plans/IRA's · · · · · · · · · · · · · · 103
      1. Qualified Plans · 103
      2. Individual Retirement Accounts · · · · · · · · · · · · · · 106
      3. Federal Tax Claims · 107
   E. Other Exemptions · 107
      1. Life Insurance · 107
      2. Miscellaneous Exemptions · · · · · · · · · · · · · · · · · · 108

VII. **OFFSHORE TRUST ENVIRONMENT — OVERVIEW OF SELECTED JURISDICTIONS** · · · · · · · · · · · · · · · · 109
   A. Common-Law Jurisdictions · 109
      1. Cook Islands · 109
         a. General information. · 109
         b. Legislation and other items of note. · · · · · · · · · · · 110
      2. Cayman Islands · 110
         a. General information. · 110
         b. Legislation and other items of note. · · · · · · · · · · · 111
      3. Gibraltar · 112
         a. General information. · 112
         b. Legislation and other items of note. · · · · · · · · · · · 112
      4. Isle of Man · 113
         a. General information. · 113
         b. Legislation and other items of note. · · · · · · · · · · · 113

    5. The Bahamas · 114
        a. General information. · 114
        b. Legislation and other items of note. · · · · · · · · · · · · 114
    6. Belize · 115
        a. General information. · 115
        b. Legislation and other items of note. · · · · · · · · · · · · 115
    7. Turks and Caicos Islands · 116
        a. General information. · 116
        b. Legislation and other items of note. · · · · · · · · · · · · 116
    8. Nevis · 117
        a. General information. · 117
        b. Legislation and other items of note. · · · · · · · · · · · · 118
    9. Liechtenstein · 118
        a. General information. · 118
        b. Legislation and other items of note. · · · · · · · · · · · · 119

VIII. SOURCES OF LIABILITY · 120
  A. Tort Creditors · 120
  B. Regulatory Creditors · 122
    1. Environmental Creditors · 122
    2. Other Regulatory Creditors · 123
  C. Contract Creditors · 124
  D. Marital Creditors · 124

IX. US REPORTING REQUIREMENTS · · · · · · · · · · · · · · · 125
  A. Gift Tax · 125
  B. Income Tax · 126
    1. Limited Partnership · 126
    2. Asset Protection Trust · 126

Table Of Contents

    C. Other · 126
        1. Foreign Trust Information Reporting · · · · · · · · · · · 127
            a. Form 3520. · 127
            b. Form 3520-A. · 128
            c. Form 1040NR. · 129
        2. Foreign Account & Foreign Asset Reporting · · · · · · · · 129

X. IRS SCRUTINY OF ABUSIVE TRUST
     ARRANGEMENTS · 130
    A. Definition of Abusive Trust. · · · · · · · · · · · · · · · · · · 130
    B. IRS Examples of Abusive Trust Arrangements · · · · · · · · 130
        1. The Business Trust · 131
        2. The Equipment or Service Trust · · · · · · · · · · · · · · 131
        3. The Family Residence Trust · · · · · · · · · · · · · · · · 132
        4. The Charitable Trust · 133
        5. The Final Trust · 133

XI. HOW TO SELECT AN ASSET PROTECTION
     ATTORNEY · 134

ENDNOTES · 139

Howard Rosen, rated "AV Preeminent"* in Martindale-Hubbell's® peer-review process, is listed in the Bar Register of Preeminent Lawyers. He holds a BBA, University of Miami (1969, magna cum laude); JD, University of Miami School of Law (1973, summa cum laude). He was a member of the editorial board, University of Miami Law Review; he is a certified public accountant, Florida; member, Florida Bar; member of BNA Tax Management Advisory Board on Estates, Gifts and Trusts (1994–present); and a member of the board of advisors of the Southpac Offshore Planning Institute (SOPI); the Asset Protection Planning Committee of the Real Property, Probate and Trust Law Section of the American Bar Association; the Tax and International Law Sections of the Florida Bar; and the American Association of Attorney-Certified Public Accountants. Mr. Rosen served as a member of the board of advisors of Aspen Publishers" *Asset Protection Journal* (1999–2001), the Board of Advisors of Warren, Gorham & Lamont"s *Journal of Asset Protection* (1995–2000), the Board of Governors of the Florida Institute of CPA's (1997-1999), as the president (1998–1999) and as a director (1991–2000) of its South Dade Chapter, and he has received the Outstanding Discussion Leader award from the Florida Institute of CPAs. He is a nationally recognized lecturer on the subjects of asset protection, taxation, and estate planning; the founding author of BNA Tax Management Portfolio, *ASSET PROTECTION PLANNING* (1994; 2002), used by lawyers, CPAs, and estate planners nationwide in researching asset protection and offshore trust issues; a contributing author of the *ABA Practical Guide To Estate Planning*: Chapter Title: "Asset Protection Trusts—What You Should Know" (2011 American Bar Association); an author of numerous articles in professional and academic journals such as the *University of Miami Law Review, Taxes Magazine,*

Journal of Taxation of Investments, University of Miami Business Law Journal, CCH Financial and Estate Planning, Tax Management *Estates, Gifts and Trusts Journal,* BNA Tax Management Portfolios, *Estate Planning, Taxation for Lawyers, Taxation for Accountants, International Tax Report, Small Business Taxation,* and others; and he is a charter member of the Planned Giving Advisory Council of the Baptist Hospital of Miami Foundation.

Patricia Donlevy-Rosen, rated "AV Preeminent"* in Martindale-Hubbell's® peer-review process, is listed in the Bar Register of Preeminent Lawyers. She holds a BA, Vassar College (1972); JD, New York Law School (1975, cum laude). She was notes and comments editor of the New York Law Forum; member of the Student Bar Association; member, Florida Bar; member, New York Bar; author, RIA Tax Advisors Planning Series publication, *ASSET PROTECTION PLANNING*, which is used by lawyers, CPAs, and estate planners nationwide in researching asset protection issues. She is the author of three chapters on asset protection in *THE BIGGEST LEGAL MISTAKES PHYSICIANS MAKE AND HOW TO AVOID THEM* (2005), published by SEAK; she authored asset protection articles published in professional and other publications such as BNA Tax Management *Estates, Gifts and Trusts Journal,* RIA's *Journal of Asset Protection,* Aspen Publishers' *Asset Protection Journal, Offshore Finance USA,* the *South Florida Business Journal,* the *Women's Business Journal,* and others. She is a member of the board of advisors of the Southpac Offshore Planning Institute (SOPI), the Estate Planning Council of Greater Miami (1995–2001), the Asset Protection Planning Committee of the Real Property, Probate and Trust Law Section of the ABA, the ABA Law Practice Management

Section Women Rainmakers Interest Group, the Business Law and Real Property, Probate and Trust Law Sections of the Florida Bar, the Florida Association of Women Lawyers, the Dade County and Coral Gables Bar Associations, and the Coral Gables Chamber of Commerce. She served as director of the New Women Entrepreneur Center Corp. (1995–1996), on the Real Property Professionalism Committee of the Real Property, Probate, and Trust Law Section of the Florida Bar (1994–1995), and on the Economics of Real Property Law Committee of the same section (1993–1994).

* AV Preeminent® is a certification mark of Reed Elsevier Properties Inc.

CHAPTER I

INTRODUCTION

The goal of this book is *not* to teach you how to do asset protection planning. The goal is to educate you as to what is necessary to properly implement an effective asset protection structure.

Ask yourself these two questions: "Am I certain my clients will never be sued?" and "Am I certain that if my clients are sued, they will be treated fairly by the US legal system?" If you answered no to either question, read on—asset protection might be appropriate for your clients.

As the twenty-first century unfolds, people are finding themselves faced with liabilities arising from sources never before imagined. Will the supermarket chain be held liable for selling red meat to Mr. Smith because he developed coronary artery disease? This may sound ludicrous, but the tobacco companies aren't laughing. Who would have thought that they would be held liable for someone's illness or death resulting from the voluntary use of their products?

Notions of asset protection have become popular fare in the media, seminars, and articles. Is asset protection something new? While the recent publicity regarding asset protection planning may be something new,[1] asset protection is not new. Trusts have been used since the time of the Crusades to protect assets, although some of the other asset protection techniques discussed in this book belong only to current times.

Personal[2] asset protection planning falls within the legal discipline of estate planning. Both traditional estate planning and asset protection planning require the lawyer (*and make no mistake, this is not do-it-yourself planning—a competent, experienced lawyer[3] must be used to properly implement your client's asset protection plan*) to utilize an analytical approach wherein the lawyer will obtain information regarding the client's financial condition, determine the client's lifetime and testamentary dispositive goals, and design and implement a plan that achieves those goals. In addition, both personal asset protection planning and conventional estate planning utilize similar tools and techniques: wills, trusts, partnerships, outright gifts, gifts in trust, and so on. The traditional goal of the estate planner in implementing a client's goals has been to preserve and protect the client's assets for the benefit of the client's family and other beneficiaries *following the client's death*—reducing transfer taxes and avoiding probate costs and delays; asset protection planning expands this respectable endeavor to include **preserving and protecting your client's assets for the client's own use and benefit** during the client's lifetime.

A. <u>Definition of Asset Protection Planning</u>

For purposes of this book, unless otherwise indicated by the context, the term "asset protection planning" (APP) will mean the adoption of advance planning techniques that tend to place your client's assets beyond the reach of future potential creditors, while your client *continues to benefit from those assets*.[4] APP *must not* involve hiding assets or committing fraud, perjury, or tax evasion.

Introduction

B. Traditional Asset Protection Methods and Their Inherent Problems

1. Outright Gifts

Utilizing the asset protection maxim, "If you don't own it, it can't be taken away from you," outright gifts *do* effect an asset protection result, although a true[5] outright gift is seldom made with asset protection in mind. The "cost" of this type of asset protection includes the loss of the income and appreciation from the gifted property, the loss of the management and control of the gifted property, the exposure of the gifted property to the donee's[6] creditors, and depending upon the identity of the donee and the nature of the property, the potential for gift tax consequences.[7]

2. Gifts in Trust—General

While a gift to a *revocable* trust results in virtually no asset protection for the settlor/donor,[8] it may, with careful drafting, provide some protection for other beneficiaries of the trust.[9] A gift to an *irrevocable* trust can accomplish an asset protection result similar to an outright gift if the settlor is not a beneficiary of the trust and has retained no control over the trust. As with the outright gift, the settlor[10] must actually part with the income from and the control over the assets transferred to the trust. In addition, depending upon the provisions of the trust and the identity of its beneficiaries, gift tax issues (for the settlor) may accompany the creation of an irrevocable trust. Unlike an outright gift, however, while the gifted assets are held in a ***properly drafted trust***, the assets can be protected from the beneficiaries' (donees') creditors.[11] The use of trusts in APP will be discussed in greater detail in section IV below.

3. Co-Ownership of Property—aka Concurrent Estates

In this section on co-ownership of property, the terms "tenant," "tenants," "tenancy," "cotenancy," and similar derivatives are used. The reader should read such terms to mean "owner" and derivatives of that word.

a. Tenancies by the entireties.

A tenancy by the entireties is a special form of co-ownership that can only be created during marriage and exist between a husband and wife. In its traditional form, a tenancy by the entireties was "not unilaterally severable" by the husband or the wife[12]—that meant that neither the husband nor the wife, *acting alone*, could transfer or encumber the property (both had to sign). As a result, in those states that follow the foregoing traditional rule, the creditor of one spouse cannot execute upon (take) property held in this form.[13]

Since tenancies by the entireties can only be created between spouses, the creation of this form of ownership will not usually result in gift tax consequences, since transfers between spouses are generally eligible for the unlimited gift tax marital deduction provided in the Internal Revenue Code (the "Code").[14] **However**, it is important to understand that any asset protection afforded by this form of ownership will disappear in the event of divorce or death, unless, in the case of death, the decedent is the debtor spouse, or in the case of a divorce, the property is awarded to the non-debtor spouse.[15] If you are thinking about using tenancy by the entireties as an asset protection technique, you should be cognizant of the *transitory nature of the protection afforded*.

b. <u>Joint tenancy with right of survivorship (JTWROS).</u>

This form of co-ownership provides minimal (if any) asset protection at best. At common law,[16] this form of ownership was unilaterally severable by either co-owner;[17] therefore, if you and I owned a parcel of land as joint tenants with right of survivorship, I could sell my portion to anyone I like, without your permission; that's what "unilaterally severable" means. That term also implies that the creditor of any co-owner under this form of co-ownership can reach the property interest of such co-owner.[18] Thus, your creditor can reach your portion, and my creditor can reach my portion. The creation of a JTWROS may result in a taxable gift, depending upon the identity of the new co-owner(s) and the nature of the property involved.[19] In addition, the creation of a joint tenancy exposes the property interest of the new joint owner to his or her creditors as well as the creditors of the original owner.[20] This form of co-ownership is often implemented to avoid probate, without thought being given to the other, negative consequences, of that action.

> **Example:** Grandmother wants to avoid probate, and instead of utilizing a trust arrangement, she conveys Blackacre Farm to herself and her grandson as joint tenants with right of survivorship. Grandson becomes involved in litigation, and a judgment is entered against him. Grandson's creditor can reach grandson's property interest in Blackacre Farm. (An even worse result occurs if the grandmother dies, in which case the grandson's creditor will be entitled to all of Blackacre Farm to satisfy his judgment.)

If any asset protection is afforded through the use of this form of ownership, it would be that during the lifetimes of the joint owners, a creditor of one joint owner can only reach that person's fractional interest in the property, and if the *indebted* joint owner dies before the creditor has perfected his claim to the property, the creditor will be unsuccessful in reaching this property.[21]

    c. <u>Tenants in common.</u>

At common law, each tenant in common owned an undivided fractional share of the property, and the interest of each co-owner was unilaterally severable and devisable (transferable) in a will. Thus, the creditor of a co-owner could reach that debtor-co-owner's undivided fractional interest in the property, and since survivorship is not an element of this form of cotenancy (as it is above), the death of the debtor-co-owner will *not* terminate the ability of his creditors to reach his interest. Thus, any asset protection available (for the transferor) by the creation of this form of ownership would parallel that discussed in section B 1 above (outright gifts), as would the gift tax consequences, with respect to the transferred undivided interest.

    4. <u>Other</u>

Other methods of asset protection have involved concealing assets, and variations of "asset return" arrangements under which the donee informally (unofficially) agrees to hold title to the donor-debtor's assets until the creditor problem goes away.

Example: Dr. Quatro, concerned that he may be sued for malpractice, gives his stamp collection to his elderly, retired aunt Cindy, who doesn't appear likely to incur liabilities. Unbeknownst to Dr. Quatro, Aunt Cindy has cosigned a loan for one of her ne'er-do-well nephews

Introduction

(who defaults on the loan), and the lender turns to Aunt Cindy to pay up. When her liquid assets are insufficient to pay the nephew's creditor, the lender looks to the valuable stamp collection - and takes it away. Another possibility: Aunt Cindy dies, and the stamp collection becomes part of her probate estate, and any "agreement" to return the stamps to Dr. Quatro disappears with Aunt Cindy. In addition, to be effective, these methods would require one or more persons to commit the crime of perjury. An ethical attorney cannot assist anyone in committing a crime. Effective APP will *not* be based upon secret arrangements, nor will it be based upon fraud. The assumption should be that *everything is discoverable. Nothing is secret.*

CHAPTER II

LIMITED PARTNERSHIPS

Limited partnerships have existed in the United States since the first limited partnership statute was adopted by New York in 1822.[22] Limited partnerships have been extensively used (*overused*) as a stand-alone asset protection strategy.

Since 1916, a number of Uniform Limited Partnership Acts have been enacted. The latest version, the Uniform Limited Partnership Act (2001) (ULPA), has been adopted by eighteen states and the District of Columbia.[23]

A. Asset Protection Aspects

There are two facets to the asset protection afforded by the use of a limited partnership. The first, widely known facet, is the "inside-out" protection available to the limited partners. This asset protection aspect can be identical[24] to the protection generally available to a corporate shareholder and a member of a limited liability company: a limited partner's personal exposure for the debts of the partnership is generally limited to his investment in the partnership.[25] That means a creditor of the partnership cannot go after the personal assets of a limited partner in order to satisfy the partnership's debt.[26] However, a partnership's creditor can go after the personal assets of the general partner. Thus, a corporation is often used as a general partner.

The second asset protection facet of the limited partnership is two pronged: one prong is arguably provided by the Internal Revenue Service (discussed in II A 2, below), and the other prong is provided by the "outside-in" protection afforded by the charging order concept. Under the charging order concept of the ULPA, discussed below, partnership assets ("inside") are protected from the personal judgment creditors[27] ("outside") of *both* the limited and the general partners.[28] This result becomes more meaningful in a limited partnership whose partners include only your client, your client's immediate family, and entities created by them, whereby a significant portion of the family wealth can be provided substantial protection from untoward future events by merely changing its form of ownership into a limited partnership form.

1. Charging Order Concept

a. Background and history.

The general concept of the charging order has been around for about one hundred years. A charging order provision is found in the Uniform Partnership Act of 1914 (UPA), the Uniform Partnership Act of 1992, the Uniform Limited Partnership Act of 1916, and in the ULPA. The provision and its effect are somewhat different in each of the Acts, and the planner must be cognizant of these differences. In addition, the implementation of the ULPA by the adopting jurisdictions may not be identical to the ULPA language (sometimes minor changes are made by a state adopting a uniform law).

The ULPA allows the foreclosure (taking by a partner's creditor) of the partnership interest subject to the charging order.[29] This is a significant change from the prior uniform limited partnership act (which did not permit foreclosure) and is viewed by the authors as an erosion of the protection previously afforded partners of a limited partnership formed under that prior law.

    b. <u>Definition.</u>

A charging order is a statutory means of providing a creditor with a procedure for collecting a judgment debt owed by a partner.[30] That means that if you had a judgment against Mr. First, and his only asset was his partnership interest in XYZ, Limited Partnership, the applicable charging order law would set forth the manner by which you would collect your judgment. It is the exclusive remedy for a judgment creditor of a partner in a limited partnership.[31] The creditor holding the charging order is *not* entitled to participate in the management or conduct of the limited partnership's activities, obtain access to information concerning the limited partnership's transactions, or inspect or copy the limited partnership's other records. Thus, the charging order holding creditor does not become a partner or have the legal ability to exercise any rights of a partner.

    c. <u>Effect of charging order.</u>

The effect of the charging order is that the partner's judgment creditor will receive those partnership distributions that would, absent the charging order, have been distributed to the debtor partner, *if, as, and when* such distributions are made. If the debtor partner is a partner in a publicly traded or other widely held limited partnership that regularly makes distributions, the charging order may be an effective means for the judgment creditor to collect part or all of his or her judgment. However, where the debtor partner is a member of a family or other closely held limited partnership governed by a *properly drafted* limited partnership agreement, the result can (and often will) be quite different, since significantly greater control over distributions will exist.

d. Summary.

In summary, a creditor with a charging order has none of the rights of a partner in the limited partnership[32] and is only entitled to the distributions that the debtor partner would have received. It is not clear how the creditor's ability to foreclose on the debtor partner's interest would be beneficial to the creditor in the family limited partnership context. A limited partnership agreement focused on asset protection should contain language that would avoid distributions to and otherwise limit the rights attendant to a "charged" partnership interest. However, one cannot be certain that a result-oriented US court would uphold such limiting provisions.

2. What Does the Internal Revenue Service Say about Charging Orders?

The above charging order material discusses the treatment of a partner's judgment creditor under state property law. This section discusses how the Internal Revenue Service might view the charging order relationship.

A closely held or family limited partnership agreement will almost always contain a provision requiring a partner intending to transfer a partnership interest to obtain the consent of the general partner (and possibly that of a majority of the limited partners) prior to the transfer in order for the transferee to be accepted as a substitute partner.

In Revenue Ruling 77-137,[33] the Internal Revenue Service said that where a limited partnership agreement contained that type of requirement, and it was not complied with, that a transferee would nevertheless be treated as a partner for *federal income tax purposes*, where the transferee acquired substantially all of the dominion and control over the partnership interest. The ruling states that under the irrevocable assignment in issue, the transferee would share in the profits and losses of the partnership and receive all distributions, including liquidating distributions to which the transferor limited partner would have been entitled had the transfer not been made.

The ruling held that the assignee would be required to report on his tax return the share of the partnership income, loss, gain, deduction, and credit attributable to the assigned interest, in the same manner as would be required if the assignee were a substitute limited partner. *This would be the case even if no distributions were actually made.* Thus, the thinking is that a judgment creditor holding a charging order may be required to report on his tax return a portion of partnership profits, even if no cash was distributed to him. An awkward position at best, and thought by some to be a deterrent to a creditor to obtain a charging order.

B. US Tax Consequences of Creation and Use of Limited Partnerships

1. Income Tax

a. Creation of limited partnership.

In general, no gain or loss is recognized to a partnership or to any of its partners upon the contribution of property to the partnership in exchange for a partnership interest, or as an additional contribution by a partner with respect to his interest in the partnership.[34]

As with any general rule, this one has its numerous exceptions. However, most of these will not be relevant in the context of the family limited partnership, particularly since the primary objective in its use as an asset protection vehicle is not tax motivated.

The exception that may be of concern in this context is the "investment company" exception.[35] This exception to the tax-free formation of a partnership would apply, for example, where the family members (partners) each contribute their separate portfolios of different marketable securities to the partnership with the thought that the formation of the partnership in this manner would effectively diversify each partner's securities holdings. If this exception applied, each partner would be treated as having sold his securities portfolio at market value and would be liable for income tax on the gains.

b. <u>Ongoing use of limited partnership.</u>

Absent any special allocation provisions in the partnership agreement, each of the partners, general and limited, will be required to report on his or her income tax return his or her allocable share (percentage) of partnership income, deductions, and credits.[36]

In some circumstances, it may be advisable for the general partner (or partners) to receive a "guaranteed payment" (a sort of management fee) from the partnership for services rendered in managing the partnership assets.[37] The guaranteed payment would be included in the gross income of the recipient partner (regardless of the partnership operating results) and would constitute a deduction at the partnership level, which would be allocated to all the partners in accordance with their partnership percentages.[38]

Limited Partnerships

As long as the focus of the partnership agreement is on asset preservation and not on gaining an undue tax advantage, no particular problems should arise in connection with the operation of the limited partnership.

2. <u>Estate/Gift Tax</u>

The estate and gift tax consequences of the establishment and use of the limited partnership will depend upon the ultimate ownership structure. For example, if a husband and wife transfer property to a family limited partnership and receive in exchange for their transfers general and limited partnership interests of equivalent value, there will be no estate or gift tax consequence. Even assuming one spouse contributed all of the property in exchange for partnership interests received by both spouses, it is likely that, absent unusual circumstances, the gift of the partnership interest (general or limited) to the noncontributing spouse will qualify for the gift tax annual exclusion and the gift tax marital deduction so that no gift tax would be imposed.[39] Where partnership interests will be transferred to a noncontributing partner who is not the spouse of the contributing partner (like children), the gift tax consequences will depend upon various factors.

If the recipient is an individual other than the spouse of the contributing partner, the annual exclusion will be available, and the value of the gift in excess of the annual exclusion will be subject to the gift tax,[40] although a valuation discount may be allowed (reducing the value of the gift).[41]

If the recipient is a trust, the transfers to which are treated as completed gifts, the availability of the annual exclusions will depend upon whether the trust instrument includes withdrawal powers for the trust beneficiaries sufficient to render the gift to the trust eligible for the annual exclusion (as a present interest gift).[42]

If the recipient is a trust, the transfers to which are not treated as completed transfers (for whatever reason), no gift tax consequence would attach to the transfer.[43]

CHAPTER III

LIMITED LIABILITY COMPANIES

A. Background

The limited liability company (LLC) is a statutory entity available in every state, the District of Columbia, and in a number of offshore jurisdictions.[44]

The common characteristics of the LLC are that its owners are called "members," it is governed by an "operating agreement," "articles of organization," and "regulations," and it may be managed on a day-to-day basis by "member(s)" or "manager(s)."

B. Asset Protection Aspects

Although the various limited liability company statutes are far from uniform, most do contain a charging order provision.

Under the 2006 Revised Uniform Limited Liability Company Act, the charging order provision has essentially the same legal consequences discussed above with respect to the ULPA charging order. What is missing, however, is a body of case law such as exists with respect to limited partnerships. From an "inside-out" liability perspective (see section II A, above), the LLC is *inherently* superior to the typical limited partnership, in that no LLC member is exposed to the internal liabilities of the LLC, which may be particularly important where the entity will hold an asset such as real estate that is capable of generating its own liability. Recall that in a limited partnership, the personal assets of the general partner are exposed to partnership liabilities. This distinction may not be important where the entity (limited partnership or limited liability company) will be used to hold marketable securities, as it would seem unlikely that holding that type of asset would generate a liability (compared to holding a rental property, which could generate a liability).

The use of the LLC in asset protection, however, will likely be restricted until a uniform statute is adopted in a majority (if not all) of the states. Otherwise, unless the activities and property ownership of the LLC will be restricted to only include the state in which it is organized, the treatment of an LLC member vis-à-vis his creditors and the creditors of the LLC will be uncertain in a state that does not have an identical LLC statute or a statute recognizing foreign LLCs.[45] Such uncertainty is contrary to one of the primary purposes of asset protection—to reduce or eliminate risk and uncertainty.

C. US Tax Consequences of Creation and Use of Limited Liability Companies

1. Income Tax

The federal income tax consequences of the creation and use of the LLC will depend upon whether it is classified as a partnership, a corporation, or as a disregarded entity. In any case, however, the creation of the entity will generally be tax-free.

Depending upon a tax election (or default IRS classification), an LLC may be classified as either a partnership, a corporation, or in the case of a single-member LLC, a "disregarded" entity for US income tax purposes.[46] Multimember LLCs are usually classified as partnerships for federal income tax purposes.

a. Treatment as a partnership:

If the LLC is treated as a partnership, the income tax consequences of its operation will be as set forth above in section II B 1 b.

b. Treatment as a corporation:

The operational tax consequences of the LLC being treated as a corporation will depend to some extent on whether it is treated as a C corporation or as an S corporation. An S corporation generally pays no income tax itself, because its earnings are reported on the personal income tax return of its shareholder(s) either as salary or as dividends. The net income of a C corporation, on the other hand, is subject to tax at the corporate level, and any payments to its shareholders will be taxable as either salary or as dividends (the corporation does not get a deduction for dividend payments, so the only way to reduce the taxable income of the corporation is to make salary payments).

c. Treatment as a disregarded entity:

If the LLC is treated as a disregarded entity, its operational results will be reported on the income tax return of its "tax owner."[47] Whether the LLC is foreign or domestic, the nature of the LLC's income and the type of tax owner will determine the specific manner of reporting the LLC's income.

2. Estate/Gift Tax

Whether the LLC is treated as a partnership or as a corporation, the estate and gift tax consequences will be as outlined in section II B 2, above.

CHAPTER IV

TRUSTS

Aside from any protection available under state exemption laws, limited partnerships, and limited liability companies (if you believe such laws or entities will protect you), a trust will be the cornerstone of any effective asset protection plan. A trust is a legal relationship (usually set forth in a written document, but it can be oral) in which one person holds legal title to property, subject to an obligation to hold, operate, invest, or use (administer) the property for the benefit of another. A trust will involve three parties at a minimum (in non-asset protection trusts one person could possibly be all three): the settlor (also called trustor, grantor, trustmaker, or creator) – this is the person who creates the trust; the trustee – a person or company who/that administers the trust; and the beneficiaries - the persons for whose benefit the trust was created and is administered. Offshore trusts will usually have a fourth party: the protector (also called the enforcer). As this is not a traditional role at common law, the trust document should specify the powers and duties of the protector (the laws of some countries set forth default powers and duties that will apply if not otherwise specified in the trust document). The primary role of the protector in offshore trust planning will be to oversee the administration of the trust by the trustee – sort of a "check and balance" arrangement. The protector will often have the power to veto any discretionary act the trustee desires to undertake (thus requiring the trustee to obtain permission in advance), and the protector will often have the power to remove and replace the trustee.

The IRS definition of a trust recognizes the centuries-old core purpose of a trust by defining a trust as "…an arrangement…whereby trustees take title to property for *the purpose of conserving and protecting it for the beneficiaries*…[who] may be the persons who create [the trust]." That sounds great. So why can't a self-created protective trust be established right here in the United States?

In most common-law jurisdictions (including the United States), this traditional protective characteristic of the trust has been eroded over the past several hundred years by evolving public policy. These erosions are (examples follow)

1. <u>Retained Powers/Controls.</u>

Under a rule derived from this public policy, if a settlor (the person who creates the trust) retains extensive powers or controls over a trust, a court could say that the trust was invalid from its inception, because the trustee is supposed to be in control of the trust, not the settlor. If the trust were found to be invalid, a creditor could reach the trust assets because the assets would be deemed to have never been transferred to the trust (that is, they still belong to the settlor).

2. <u>Self-Settled Spendthrift Trust.</u>

A spendthrift trust is a trust that contains a "spendthrift" provision. A spendthrift provision is language in the trust that prevents a beneficiary from transferring, selling, or pledging his interest in the trust, and these features are thought of as being protective in nature.

Another aspect of general US trust law is that a person (settlor) cannot establish a spendthrift trust for his or her own benefit and obtain any asset protection benefit from the spendthrift aspect of the trust.

3. Creditor Accessibility Rule (aka "maximum potential interest rule").

Finally, under our protection-eroded general US trust law, a settlor's creditor can reach trust assets to the extent that the trustee of the trust would be permitted to distribute assets to the settlor under the terms of the trust document. Thus, if a settlor creates a trust in which the settlor and other persons are designated as beneficiaries, and the trust also provides that it is totally the trustee's decision whether, to which beneficiary, and how much to distribute (a "discretionary trust"), the settlor's creditor would be able to reach the entire trust, since the trustee could, under the terms of the trust document, distribute that much to the settlor (in the settlor's capacity as a beneficiary).

A. Trusts in Non-Community Property Jurisdictions

1. Asset Protection Aspects

As mentioned above, trusts have been used since the time of the Crusades to protect assets, and they are still being used, and now publicized, in asset protection matters. The authors consider the trust concept to be an "inherent" legal concept in the common-law legal system. This means that lawyers in every common-law country were taught the same basic principles of trust law. Thus, the predictability and stability of the use of trusts in a common-law jurisdiction. In this section, the primary focus will be on the asset protection aspects of *trusts for the benefit of the settlor (i.e., where the settlor is designated as a beneficiary)*, although other aspects will be addressed. Fraudulent transfer issues, regarding trusts and other transfers, are discussed in section V, below.

    a. Domestic trusts

        i. Working definition.

For purposes of this discussion, we will define a "domestic trust" to be a trust, the construction, operation, and administration of which is governed by the laws of any state, US territory or possession, the District of Columbia, or of the United States.

        ii. Discussion.

The efficacy of a domestic trust in providing asset protection depends upon the relationship to the trust of the person for whom asset protection is sought, and the nature and extent of that person's interest in and/or controls over the trust. For example, a trust that is revocable by the settlor, even one under which the settlor is not a beneficiary, provides virtually no protection from the claims of the settlor's creditors during the settlor's lifetime,[48] although some early cases held to the contrary.[49] The authors proceed on the assumption that a court will allow the creditors of the settlor of a domestic revocable trust access to the trust assets.[50] Access to domestic revocable trust assets would be gained by a creditor via a court order on the settlor to revoke or partially revoke the trust, or via an order on the trustee to distribute trust assets to pay the settlor's creditor.

Following the settlor's death, and even though the revocable trust assets are generally not probate assets, some states may permit the creditors of the settlor's probate estate to reach the assets of a trust over which the settlor had a retained power of revocation.[51]

A trust that is revocable by the settlor, but whose beneficiaries are persons other than the settlor, is capable of providing asset protection benefits with respect to the *non-settlor-beneficiaries*.[52]

> Example 1: Settlor A establishes a trust under which he retains a power of revocation, designating B and C as beneficiaries of the trust. Under the terms of the trust, the trustee (who is neither B nor C) has the discretion to "pay or apply the whole, any portion, or none of the trust income and/or principal to or for the benefit of B or C, to the exclusion of one or both of them." B and C's creditors cannot reach the trust income or principal, unless and until it is distributed to them, because the quoted language does not create a reachable property interest (until distributed).[53] This is an example of a discretionary trust provision, discussed in greater detail below. Note: Settlor A's creditors can reach the trust assets.

Even if the settlor's specific intent in including such a provision in the trust was to deny recovery against the trust assets to the non-settlor-beneficiary's creditor, it will be upheld.[54]

If a revocable trust provides no protection for the settlor from his or her creditors, what degree of protection *for the settlor* can be expected from a domestic *irrevocable* trust? The answer to this question: It depends. It depends upon the nature and extent of the other "strings" the settlor has retained with respect to the trust. Even where various strings, taken separately, might not allow a court to permit the settlor's creditor access to trust assets, such strings, viewed in the aggregate, might amount to sufficient dominion and control in the settlor to permit a court to allow his creditors to reach trust assets.[55] In addition, some trust provisions that will protect non-settlor-beneficiaries will not be permitted to protect the settlor-beneficiary on public policy grounds.

> Example 2: Settlor A establishes an irrevocable trust, naming himself and D as discretionary income and principal beneficiaries, and naming E as trustee. In example 1, above, we saw that such a discretionary distribution provision could effectively protect the trust assets from the creditors of non-settlor-beneficiaries - even in a revocable trust. However, for public policy reasons, such a provision will not be effective to insulate the assets of the domestic trust from the creditors of the *settlor*, who is also a beneficiary. In general, the creditors of this settlor-beneficiary will be able to reach that amount of trust income and/or principal that the trustee, in the maximum exercise of its discretion in favor of the settlor-beneficiary, could pay or apply for the benefit of the settlor-beneficiary under the terms of the trust.[56] Thus, where a trustee is given unfettered discretion in making distributions to a settlor-beneficiary or to a non-settlor-beneficiary, the law assumes that the trustee would distribute the entire trust (based on the language in this example) to the settlor-beneficiary and, therefore, that is the amount

the settlor-beneficiary's creditor can reach - *the entire trust.*

The same rule applies to an irrevocable trust established by the settlor for his support.[57]

Similarly, for public policy reasons, a properly drafted spendthrift provision (discussed below), which generally insulates trust assets from the creditors of a *non*-settlor beneficiary, will *not be effective* in protecting trust assets from the creditors of a settlor-beneficiary.[58]

> Example 3: Settlor A establishes an irrevocable trust, naming himself as the income and principal beneficiary. The trust sets forth that it is a spendthrift trust.[59] Although a spendthrift trust would generally protect trust income and principal from the creditors of a non-settlor-beneficiary,[60] the provision will be ineffective in protecting the <u>domestic</u> trust from the creditors of the settlor-beneficiary.[61]

The foregoing material should not be taken to mean that asset protection planning is unavailable for the settlor of a domestic trust. What the material does mean is that the maximum property interest *potentially* available to the settlor under his or her domestic trust will also be available to satisfy the claims of the settlor's creditors via a court order to that effect on the trustee (or, in the case of a revocable trust, an order on the settlor). Given this, consider the following examples.

> Example 4: Settlor A establishes an irrevocable trust, naming himself as the <u>income</u> beneficiary

(discretionary or required—we've seen that for asset protection planning purposes, it doesn't matter), and retaining a power to appoint (direct the distribution of) trust principal to and among his three children. The trust provides that if A does not exercise this power, the trust principal will be distributed at A's death to his children equally. A's creditors can reach A's income interest (because the income is available to A); however, since A no longer has a beneficial interest in <u>trust principal</u>, other than the special power of appointment, his creditors will be unsuccessful in reaching the trust principal. Note: A has really given away the principal.

<u>Example 5:</u> Mrs. W establishes an irrevocable trust, naming herself as the income beneficiary, and granting the trustee the discretion to distribute principal to her, if the trust income, together with Mrs. W's other resources, are insufficient to provide for her reasonable support, medical care, and comfort. Unless the trustee abuses its discretion, the settlor's creditors will not be able to reach the trust principal.

Because the principal distributions to the settlor have been limited to an ascertainable standard (as compared to granting the trustee unfettered discretion), the settlor's creditors, in order to reach the trust principal, would be required to prove that the standard had been satisfied (i.e., in example 5, above, that the trust income and the settlor's other resources were insufficient to provide for the settlor's reasonable support, medical care, and comfort), so that the trustee's failure to distribute principal under such circumstances was improper.[62]

iii. State asset protection trust laws.

Having observed these deficiencies in general US trust law, and seeking to obtain potential trust business, the legislatures of a number of states (most notably Alaska and Delaware) have enacted varying degrees of asset protection trust legislation. Generally, such legislation purportedly permits a settlor of a trust to be a discretionary beneficiary of a trust and obtain the desired asset protection advantages (that is, the above erosionary rules will not apply).[63] For numerous reasons, the effectiveness of such domestic asset protection laws is highly questionable. In the *Huber* case (2013), a Washington State resident established an Alaska "asset protection" trust. The settlor ended up in a federal bankruptcy court in Washington state, and, not surprisingly, the trust failed to protect the his assets for a couple of reasons. First, the federal court held that Washington law, which does not permit asset protection trusts, applied; thus, no protection was available for Mr. Huber - because the federal bankruptcy court could order the Alaska trustee company to give back the assets. Second, and very importantly, section 548(e)(1) of the bankruptcy law permits the bankruptcy court to "undo" any such trust for a period of <u>ten years</u> after it is established, and so it was. These rules were effective to dismantle the Alaska trust for <u>one reason</u>: the Alaska trustee - who held title to trust assets - was subject to the jurisdiction (power) of the US court system. This means that the Alaska trustee (or any other US-based trustee) had to comply with the order of the federal court or be held in contempt. We'll see below how an offshore trust is different.

Issues Affecting/Limiting the Asset Protection Aspects of Domestic Asset Protection Trusts:

I. The Full Faith and Credit Clause of the US Constitution provides that "Full Faith and Credit shall be given in each State to the public Acts, Records, and judicial Proceedings of every other State..." Full faith and credit principles are so broadly construed that they generally require the judgment of another state to be recognized and enforced, even though the original claim is illegal in, or contrary to the strong public policy of, the second state. In addition, the Full Faith and Credit Clause is also usually thought to require the enforcement of another state's judgments, even where the second state disallows by statute jurisdiction over the action. In fact, assuming that in personam jurisdiction is obtained over the trustee, there are only two apparent limitations upon the application of the Full Faith and Credit Clause. The first limitation upon application of the Full Faith and Credit Clause is that "... for a State's substantive law to be selected in a constitutionally permissible manner, that State must have a significant contact or significant aggregation of contacts, creating state interests, such that choice of its law is neither arbitrary nor fundamentally unfair." The second limitation upon application of the Full Faith and Credit Clause is that the issue has been fully and fairly litigated and finally decided in the court rendering the original judgment. By way of sharp comparison, many foreign jurisdictions will not recognize the judgments of US courts.

II. The Supremacy Clause of the US Constitution, which generally provides for the supremacy of federal law over state law when and wherever the two shall conflict, also significantly diminishes the protection provided by a state's asset protection legislation, since it will always remain subject to the potential superseding application of federal law to the contrary. Most significantly, especially in view of the Bankruptcy Abuse Prevention and Consumer Protection Act of 2005, this includes the US Bankruptcy Code (see above).

III. The Contract Clause of the US Constitution prohibits the enactment of any state law that impairs the obligations of parties to contracts. Thus, legislation that precludes the enforcement of judgments against property that remains for the beneficial use of the settlor/debtor is arguably unconstitutional.

iv. Summary.

The domestic trust, if used for asset protection purposes, must be used with an understanding of its above-described limitations. The reader must bear in mind the general rule that "the creditor of a beneficiary under a trust has the same rights and can secure the same benefits from a trust as the beneficiary himself,"[64] and that a settlor cannot create an effective spendthrift trust for his or her own benefit (except, purportedly, in the "asset protection" trust states). To the extent the settlor's interest in the trust is restricted or eliminated, the settlor has lost a property interest. To some, this is acceptable, to others, it is not.

In utilizing the domestic planning techniques discussed above, the planner must take care not to convert a trust provision that might be effective in protecting trust principal from the settlor's creditors (see examples 4 and 5, above) into a spendthrift or unfettered discretionary provision that will not be effective.

b. Offshore (Foreign Situs) Trusts

i. Working definition.

For purposes of the following discussion, an "offshore trust" is one under which at least one trustee is resident outside of the United

States (and its territories and possessions), and that is construed, interpreted, administered, and otherwise subject to the laws of a foreign country (usually, but not necessarily, the same country where the non-US trustee is resident). NOTE: The term "offshore trust" is *not* a tax law term, since an offshore trust may be a "foreign trust" (the tax law term) or a US trust for US income tax purposes, depending upon its structure.

ii. Discussion.

In the above discussion of the asset protection aspects of domestic trusts, it was stated that the ability of a domestic trust to provide effective asset protection depended upon the relationship to the trust of the person for whom protection was sought (i.e., settlor-beneficiary or non-settlor-beneficiary), and the nature and extent of that person's interest in and/or controls over the trust. To a significant extent, the protection afforded through the use of a properly drafted and situated offshore asset protection trust (APT) will *not* depend upon these factors.

The APT is *inherently more protective* for several reasons, not the least of which is its "foreignness." Consider the thought processes of the creditor's attorney contemplating a court action to recover assets from a trust in a foreign country. He knows nothing of their geography, laws, procedures, costs, or even their currency. These factors become immediate hurdles in a legal obstacle course upon which he is about to embark. Because of these geographical, legal, procedural, and financial hurdles, the APT is not an automatic target of litigation, as its domestic counterpart would likely be. The domestic trust and its trustees are subject to US court jurisdiction (power), and both are just as easily included in litigation (on some legal theory or another) as is the settlor—not so with the APT. The very fact that the APT is an offshore trust will have a significant deterrent effect on the creditor's decision regarding to what extent (or even whether) to pursue trust assets. Finally, as will be discussed in section iii (B) below, the trust laws of certain foreign jurisdictions are far more specific and protective than are our domestic trust laws. Therefore, if the creditor is (somehow) undaunted by the geographical, financial, and procedural hurdles of the APT obstacle course, he will be confronted with the brick wall of the foreign legal system as the final hurdle.

iii. Selecting the APT jurisdiction.

The first step in the process of implementing an APT is selecting an appropriate jurisdiction for the location of the trust (referred to as the "situs" of the trust). Among the factors to consider in selecting the jurisdiction for the APT are

(A) <u>Legal System.</u> A jurisdiction whose legal system is English common law-based will have an inherent trust concept and legal foundation upon which APT planning can be reliably structured. Contrast the English common law-based system with a system based upon the civil law (sometimes referred to as the Napoleonic Code), which does not contain an indigenous trust concept.[65]

Some civil law jurisdictions, such as the Channel Islands[66] and Liechtenstein, have enacted legislation establishing the trust concept in their respective legal systems. Some planners suggest that the use of an appropriate civil law jurisdiction as the situs of the APT adds another protective aspect to the structure: the creditor's attorney will encounter additional difficulty in comprehending and may be daunted by a civil law legal system that incorporates a trust concept. Because of US tax law entity classification issues, with attendant potential property and tax law bombshells,[67] however, one must determine whether these risks are worth the possible tenuous benefit suggested in the preceding sentence, particularly when several jurisdictions offer suitable common-law systems.

Examples of common law-based jurisdictions with favorable trust legislation in place include Cook Islands, Nevis, Belize, Cyprus, Gibraltar, Isle of Man, and the Turks and Caicos Islands.

(B) Favorable Trust Protection and Tax Laws.

(I) General

In addition to being based in the English common law, the selected jurisdiction should have in place legislation establishing a set of rules specifically addressing international trusts and selected issues. Any such set of rules, or related set of rules, should address the applicability of the Statute of Elizabeth.[68]

(II) Statute of Elizabeth

In 1571, the Statute of Elizabeth (the "Statute") was enacted in England. The law enables courts to "undo" transfers of assets as "fraudulent transfers." Since its enactment, it has served as the basis for the fraudulent transfer laws of much of the civilized world. From an asset protection perspective, the problem with the Statute and its progeny has been their overly broad Draconian application.

The primary negative aspects of the Statute are that it contains *no limitation period,* and its judicial interpretations by the English courts have been detrimental to a debtor's position, typically holding that a fraudulent transfer was found where the creditor was merely deprived of timely recourse to property that would have otherwise been available for his benefit. Significantly, and dovetailing with the lack of a limitations period in the Statute, *future creditors* (i.e., those who came into existence as creditors following a transfer) could attack a transaction, making it virtually impossible for any significant asset protection planning to be undertaken.

IMPORTANT NOTE: It is important for the reader to distinguish between a fraudulent transfer and fraud, because quite often writers discussing fraudulent transfers use the terms with a lack of specificity, so much so that one could conclude that making a fraudulent transfer was committing fraud. The law defines "fraud" as knowingly misrepresenting a material fact to induce someone to act or fail to act to his detriment - a crime. Completely different is the fraudulent transfer, which is defined as making a transfer of an asset with the intent to hinder, delay, or defeat the claim of a creditor - not a crime.[69] This is discussed in greater detail in the introduction to section V, below.

In selecting a jurisdiction (country) for the establishment of the APT, the planner should look for a jurisdiction that has enacted legislation repealing the Statute, either expressly[70] or by implication.[71] Ordinarily, a statute repealing the Statute of Elizabeth will provide specific fraudulent transfer rules in its stead, including a limitations period,[72] and may require the creditor to satisfy a specific standard of proof in order to establish that a particular transfer was a fraudulent transfer.[73]

The most extensive and specific of the fraudulent transfer statutes of the offshore jurisdictions is found in §13B of the International Trusts Act 1984 (Cook Islands). The statute requires <u>the</u> complaining creditor to prove the fraudulent transfer *"beyond a reasonable doubt."* The effect of this type of fraudulent transfer provision is significant: *each* complaining creditor must endure the time and expense of proving - *beyond a reasonable doubt* - that the settlor's transfer was a fraudulent transfer <u>as to him</u>, and each such case would be required to be brought in the Cook Islands.[74]

If the settlor's assets remaining outside the trust exceed the amount of the complaining creditor's claim at the time of the complained of transfer, the settlor is "solvent" under Cook Islands law, and a fraudulent transfer case cannot be commenced in the Cook Islands; the creditor is completely out of luck. If, for some reason, the settlor was not solvent at the time of the complained of transfer, Cook Islands law contains a detailed *two-year statute of limitations,* beyond which time transfers to the trust cannot be attacked on fraudulent transfer grounds. In addition, as if proving a fraudulent transfer beyond a reasonable doubt was not difficult enough (remember the first O. J. Simpson trial?), fraudulent transfer intent may not be imputed to a settlor by reason of the fact that he has transferred property to the trust within two years of the date the creditor's cause of action accrued, or he has retained, possesses, or acquires various powers over and benefits in the trust (including the power of revocation,[75] among others), or he is a beneficiary of the trust. All of these factors would go a long way to proving a fraudulent transfer case in the United States, *but not in the Cook Islands.*

Finally, and importantly, §13B(4) of the Cook Islands trust law clearly provides that a transfer to the trust **cannot** be a fraudulent transfer as to a creditor whose cause of action arose *after* the transfer to the trust. Again, unlike the Cook Islands, in the United States, "subsequent" creditors have the ability to prove that a transfer was a fraudulent transfer.

(III) Comity.

An *extremely important* aspect of the law of any jurisdiction being considered for the situs of an APT will be the extent to which the jurisdiction adheres to the concept of "comity." *Black's Law Dictionary* defines comity, *inter alia,* as:

"[The] principle of 'comity' is that the courts of one state or jurisdiction will give effect to laws and judicial decisions of another state or jurisdiction, not as a matter of obligation but out of deference and mutual respect," and more to the point:

"Comity of nations. The recognition which one nation allows within its territory to the legislation, executive, or judicial acts of another nation, having due regard both to international duty and convenience and to the rights of its own citizens or of other persons who are under the protection of its laws."

Why is comity (or, more accurately, the *lack* of comity) such an important factor? Any order, issued by any US court, will be *entirely ineffective* where the foreign trustee of the APT is resident in a jurisdiction that does not grant comity to US judgments.

For example, §13D of the International Trusts Act 1984 (Cook Islands) clearly and specifically provides in this regard:

"13D. <u>Foreign judgements not enforceable</u>—
Notwithstanding—
(a) The provisions of any treaty;
(b) The provisions of any statute;
(c) Any rule of law, or equity, to the contrary, no proceedings for or in relation to the enforcement or recognition of a judgement obtained in a jurisdiction other than the Cook Islands against either—
(d) An international trust;
(e) A settlor of an international trust;
(f) A trustee of an international trust;

(g) A protector of an international trust;

(h) A beneficiary of an international trust;

(i) A person appointed or instructed in accordance with the express or implied provisions of an instrument or disposition to exercise a function or undertake any act, matter, or thing in connection with an international trust; or

(j) Property of either an international trust or of a trustee or a beneficiary thereof; shall be entertained by any Court in the Cook Islands if—

(k) that judgement is based upon the application of any law inconsistent with the provisions of this Act;

(l) that judgement relates to a matter or particular aspect that is governed by the law of the Cook Islands."

The importance of a lack of comity in the selected APT jurisdiction is self-evident but cannot be overemphasized.

> EXAMPLE: Creditor A sues Dr. B in state X for malpractice based upon an act committed by Dr. B several years after the establishment of his APT. The jurisdiction in which Dr. A established the APT does not recognize or give effect to foreign judgments. Creditor A is successful in his action against Dr. B in state X and obtains a judgment. In order for Creditor A to pursue the assets held by Dr. B's APT - assuming a legal theory exists upon which Creditor A can proceed against the trust assets - Creditor A will be required to commence his action *de novo* (all over again) in the courts of the APT's jurisdiction, utilizing local counsel in that country. Furthermore, since lawyers in most

(if not all) foreign jurisdictions will not accept cases on a contingency fee basis, Creditor A will be required to finance his overseas litigation as it proceeds and, in some jurisdictions, he will also be required to post a bond. *One more thing*: The case in the foreign country will not be a malpractice case - the offshore trust had nothing to do with the malpractice. Instead, the case will be a fraudulent transfer case. If the trust is a Cook Islands trust, the case cannot even be started in the Cook Islands, because Cook Islands fraudulent transfer law does not allow a "subsequent" creditor to bring a fraudulent transfer case.

(IV) <u>Effect of Retained Interests, Powers, and Self-Settled Spendthrift Provisions</u>.

Ideally, the laws of the APT jurisdiction should override the common-law rules that preclude effective asset protection for the settlor-beneficiary of a spendthrift, wholly discretionary, and certain other retained-interest trusts. An example of a statute that overrides various common-law rules that might result in a trust being declared invalid is § 13C of the International Trusts Act 1984 (Cook Islands):

"13C. <u>Retention of control and benefits by settlor</u>

An international trust...shall not be declared invalid or a disposition [a transfer to the trust] declared void or be affected in any way by reason of the fact that the settlor, and if more than one, any of them, either -

(a) Retains, possesses or acquires a power to revoke the trust ...;

(b) Retains, possesses or acquires a power of disposition over property of the trust ...;

(c) Retains, possesses or acquires a power to amend the trust ...;

(d) Retains, possesses or acquires any benefit interest or property from the trust or any disposition ...;
(e) Retains, possesses or acquires the power to remove or appoint a trustee or protector;
(f) Retains, possesses or acquires the power to direct a trustee or protector on any matter;
(g) Is a beneficiary of the trust ... either solely or together with others" (clarification supplied).

An example of a statute that overrides the common-law rule that prevents a settlor from establishing a spendthrift trust for his or her own benefit is §12 of the Trusts Act 1992 (Belize).

"Protective or spendthrift trusts

12.(1) The terms of a trust may make the interest of a beneficiary -
(a) subject to termination;
(b) subject to a restriction on alienation of or dealing in that interest or any part of that interest, or
(c) subject to diminution or termination in the event of the beneficiary becoming insolvent or any of his property becoming liable to seizure or sequestration for the benefit of his creditors and such a trust shall be known as a protective or a spendthrift trust.

(2) Where any property is directed to be held on protective or spendthrift trust for the benefit of a beneficiary, the trustee shall hold that property-
(a) in trust to pay the income to the beneficiary until the interest terminates in accordance with the terms of the trust or a determining event occurs, and
(b) if a determining event occurs, and while the interest of the beneficiary continues, in trust to pay the income to such of the

following (and if more than one in such shares) as the trustee in his absolute discretion shall appoint --
(i) the beneficiary and any spouse or child of the beneficiary; or
(ii) (if there is no such spouse or child) the beneficiary and the persons who would be entitled to the estate of the beneficiary if he had then died intestate and domiciled in Belize.

(3) In subsection (2) above, a "determining event" shall mean the occurrence of any event or any act or omission on the part of the beneficiary (other than the giving of consent to an advancement of trust property) which would result in the whole or part of the income of the beneficiary from the trust becoming payable to any person other than the beneficiary.

(4) *Any rule of law or public policy which prevents a settlor from establishing a protective or a spendthrift trust of which he is a beneficiary is hereby abolished*"(emphasis added).[76]

(V) Tax Laws; Exchange Controls.

The selected jurisdiction should exempt the APT, its assets, and its income from any type of taxation (in that jurisdiction), and from any exchange controls (in those jurisdictions that have such taxes and/or controls).

For example, §§64 and 65 of the Trusts Act 1992 (Belize) provide

"**Exemption from taxes and duties**

64.(1) For the purposes of this Act a trust shall be an exempt trust in any year if -
(a) the settlor is not resident in Belize during that year;
(b) none of the beneficiaries are resident in Belize during that year; and

(c) the trust property does not include any land situated in Belize.

(2) In any year when a trust is an exempt trust, then, notwithstanding any provision to the contrary in any enactment -
- (a) the income of the trust for that year shall be exempt from all provisions of the [BELIZE] Income Tax Act [Cap 46];
- (b) no estate, inheritance, succession or gift tax or duty shall be payable [TO BELIZE] with respect to the trust property by reason of any death occurring during that year; and
- (c) all instruments executed in that year and relating to the trust property or to transactions carried out by the trustee on behalf of the trust shall be exempt from stamp duty [IN BELIZE].

(3) In this section 'resident' shall mean resident for the purposes of the Income Tax Act (Cap 46).

Exemption from exchange control
SI 30/76

65. The trustee of an exempt trust shall be regarded as not resident in Belize for the purposes of the Exchange Control Regulations 1976 with regard to the trust property and to all transactions carried out by the trustee on behalf of the trust."[77]

(C) <u>Track Record</u>. Do the courts of the proposed jurisdiction have experience in adjudicating cases involving attacks on their asset protection trusts? If, yes, what have been the results of those cases - generally favorable to asset protection or generally not favorable to asset protection?

(D) <u>Other Factors</u>.

Other factors, which require no elaboration, to be considered in selecting the APT jurisdiction include the "health" of the economic environment, the stability of the political and social system, compatible language, availability and quality of professional and financial services, and availability and quality of electronic communication facilities.

iv. Selecting the offshore trustee.

In selecting the offshore trustee, one should seek a trust company with experience in administering APTs. Such experience should, if possible, include having "gone through the fire" of local litigation concerning an APT. One should

(A) interview the personnel of the potential trustee company to get a feel for whether personalities will be compatible with yours;

(B) inquire of the potential trustee regarding the number of APTs (and their asset value) under its administration and obtain local certificates of good standing, and (if possible), financial statements regarding the potential trust company;

(C) determine whether the potential trust company's procedures will dovetail or conflict with your procedures and obtain a schedule of fees.

Finally, it is important that the trust company have no US branch operation or other US presence. Adherence to this requirement will preclude a US court from exerting pressure on the offshore trustee through the issuance of an order on the US branch.[78] In this connection, some banks, brokerage firms, and trust companies will promote the fact that while they are based in the United States, they have an offshore subsidiary (or other related) company that is "different" than they are so that no US court can exert the pressure described above. *Do not believe this. It is just not the way things work in real life.* A related matter: What type of criteria should we consider in selecting an offshore financial institution for asset protection purposes? In addition to customary factors such as financial condition and stability, the offshore financial institution must not have any US branch, because if the offshore financial institution did have a US branch, a US court could exert some type of pressure or influence on that US branch to the detriment of your protective structure.

You may wish to visit the offshore jurisdiction in order to accomplish the foregoing due diligence.

v. How Does the Offshore Trust Work?

In order to understand how the offshore trust works to protect assets, the reader must first understand how a creditor can reach assets held in a trust. **Understanding the following is crucial to understanding how and why properly structured offshore asset protection planning works.** There are only two ways a creditor can reach assets held in a trust: the creditor must bring and win his/her case in a court that has jurisdiction (power) over the trustee, or the creditor must bring and win his/her case in a court that has jurisdiction over trust assets. If the creditor wins his/her case in a court that has jurisdiction over the trustee, the court - with the power of contempt incarceration over the trustee - will order the trustee to return the assets to the settlor so the judgment can be paid, or it will order some similar remedy with the same result. The trustee will have no choice but to comply with the court's order. If the creditor wins his/her case in a court that has jurisdiction over the trust's assets, the court can seize the assets in order to satisfy the creditor's judgment. *If* the offshore trust has been *competently* prepared and is located in an appropriate jurisdiction, no court in the United States will have jurisdiction over the trustee. It just *will not be possible for* *a US court to obtain jurisdiction over the foreign trustee.* That means that the US court will have *no power whatsoever* to force the trustee to do anything at all - period. That translates into **impenetrable protection** for liquid assets - cash and publicly traded securities - properly situated in offshore accounts held in the trust. As for US immovable assets, a US court would be able to seize such assets, which is why it is very important to implement the ancillary loan strategy discussed below well in advance of any creditor claims.

vi. Will I go to jail if I establish an offshore trust?

The short answer is no. However, because of two cases, *Anderson*[79] and *Lawrence*,[80] a Chicken Little-sky-is-falling mentality has emerged among misguided planners, uneducated planners, and those with an agenda to pursue. Civil contempt incarceration in the context of asset protection planning has been the subject of a tremendous amount of commentary. Some writers seem to have an axe to grind in this regard, as they present half-truths and innuendos as if they were the law. Most of the information is cursory and paints the contempt issue with a broad brush so that you might be led to conclude that if your client establishes an offshore asset protection trust, he/she will inevitably be incarcerated. *Nothing could be further from the truth.*

What is contempt? The law of contempt emanates from circumstances where a court orders a party to either do something or refrain from doing something, and the party disobeys. The party is then said to be "in contempt of court." Contempt can be of a criminal or civil nature, and this section will only address coercive (as opposed to remedial) civil contempt as it relates to asset protection planning. The typical coercive civil contempt sanctions are per diem fines and/or open-ended incarceration. The ***sole purpose*** of those sanctions is (and can only be) to force compliance with a court order, the theory being that the offending party can terminate the sanction by compliance with the order.

THE (ACTUAL) LAW. In order for a US court to incarcerate a party for contempt for failing to repatriate the assets of an asset protection trust when ordered to do so, the following must be proved by clear and convincing evidence: the offending party must be shown to have present possession or control of the asset sought. The burden of proof is on the party seeking to reach the asset. The seminal case in this area is *Maggio v. Zeitz*,[81] decided by the US Supreme Court in 1948 (from a long line of cases of similar holdings). Maggio addressed the impossibility of performance issue, including a self-created impossibility, and held, regarding placing assets beyond the reach of the bankruptcy court, that "...no such acts, however reprehensible, warrant issuance of an order which creates a duty impossible of performance so that punishment can follow." In other words, in order to incarcerate a party for civil contempt, it must be possible for the party to comply with the court order, and the party fails to do so. Another US Supreme Court case (Rylander[82]) followed this reasoning when the Court held in 1983 that a court cannot be blind to evidence that compliance with a court order is impossible. Many asset protection advisers are either unaware of these cases or fail to correctly understand their true meanings, as the "self-created" impossibility defense is often misunderstood. It is frequently said that impossibility of performance is a defense to a contempt citation unless the party claiming impossibility created the impossibility. That is not accurate. In order to properly advise a client on offshore trust planning, *Maggio* and *Rylander* must be accurately understood, as they continue to be the law in the United States. The fact that it can be shown that the party had possession or control of the asset sought at some prior point in time is not relevant; it must be shown that the party had possession or control at the time of the court's order or that the party created the impossibility of performance in direct anticipation or as a result of the court's order.

In the 2014 Bellinger case,[83] the plaintiff bank sought to have Mr. Bellinger incarcerated for civil contempt because he had established a Cook Islands trust during his litigation with the bank, and he was subsequently unable to pay the judgment the bank won against him. Mr. Bellinger explained that even though he knew the bank was going to try to collect on his guarantee, he was relying on indemnification agreements from his partners to satisfy his guarantee. The partners had made good on such indemnifications in the past, and Mr. Bellinger had no reason to think that they would not continue to honor their agreements. Mr. Bellinger testified, as to his reason for establishing the offshore trust, that he had recently been divorced, needed to revise and update his estate planning, and in particular, he wanted his updated estate planning to ensure the financial security of his daughter. Mr. Bellinger testified that he could not compel payment of the judgment from the trust (he had asked, and the trustee refused), that he could not replace the trustee, and that the trust was irrevocable. The court cited *Maggio*[84]: "Civil contempt orders are coercive in nature. ...To jail one for a contempt for omitting an act he is powerless to perform would reverse [that] principle and make the proceeding **purely punitive**, to describe it charitably. Contempt orders will not be issued if the court finds no willful disobedience but only an inability to comply" (emphasis supplied). Mr. Bellinger was (properly) ***not*** held in contempt.

Court decisions have consistently held that civil contempt incarceration can only be used to obtain compliance with a court order. *It cannot be used to punish,* and it can only be used when the party subject to the court order has the present ability to comply. Incarcerating a party for failing to comply with an order that is impossible to comply with is punishment and, under the law set forth by the US Supreme Court, cannot be done.

ANDERSON & LAWRENCE. In *Anderson*,[85] the settlors were the trust protectors, which, as their trust was drafted, gave them *complete control over the trust.* Their contempt incarceration was proper and resulted from poor structuring of their trust - they retained too much control over the trust. In a properly structured asset protection trust, it is **never** a good idea to permit the settlor (the creator of the trust) to retain any power over or with respect to the trust, other than a limited inter vivos or testamentary power[86] (one that can only be exercised in a will). In *Lawrence*,[87] because of discovery violations that offended the bankruptcy court, a default judgment was entered against Mr. Lawrence, and his pleadings were struck (to the same legal effect as if he had not filed pleadings in the case). As a result of the striking of his pleadings and the entry of the default judgment, Lawrence was [legally] deemed to have admitted that he had control over his trust (which he actually did, as a result of his retained power to remove and replace trustees). Since he had admitted he retained control over his trust, the bankruptcy trustee obtained a court order requiring Lawrence to "turn over" the assets of the trust to the bankruptcy trustee. When he failed to turn over the trust assets, he was incarcerated for contempt. Before the entry of the default judgment, the burden of proving by clear and convincing evidence that compliance with the turn over order was possible was on the bankruptcy trustee; once the default was entered, however, the significant burden of proving the impossibility defense (proving a negative) shifted to Mr. Lawrence. Once again, the contempt incarceration was (at least initially) proper, as the trust was incompetently drafted, giving Lawrence great control over the trust, and Lawrence had [legally] admitted control over the trust, thus, the ability to comply with the turnover order.

Consider this: Since 1984, when the Cook Islands ushered in the modern asset protection trust era, thousands and thousands of asset protection trusts have been implemented. Will you be incarcerated if you establish an offshore asset protection trust? The answer is decidedly no, *if* the trust is competently drafted and implemented at a time when there is no court order pending or anticipated.

2. US Tax Consequences

a. Domestic (US) trusts.

The income, estate, and gift tax consequences of the establishment and utilization of domestic trusts, whether as an asset protection technique or otherwise is a vast subject, and is beyond the scope of this endeavor.

b. Offshore trusts.

i. Classification issues.

(A) Trust or Something Else?

The IRS treasury regulations define a trust as follows:

> "In general, the term "trust" as used in the Internal Revenue Code refers to an arrangement created either by a will or by an inter vivos declaration *whereby trustees take title to property for the purpose of protecting or conserving it for the beneficiaries* under the

ordinary rules applied in chancery or probate courts. Usually the beneficiaries of such a trust do no more than accept the benefits thereof and are not the voluntary planners or creators of the trust arrangement. *However, the beneficiaries of such a trust may be the persons who create it, and it will be recognized as a trust under the Internal Revenue Code if it was created for the purpose of protecting or conserving the trust property for beneficiaries who stand in the same relation to the trust as they would if the trust had been created by others for them.* Generally speaking, an arrangement will be treated as a trust under the Internal Revenue Code if it can be shown that the purpose of the arrangement is to vest in trustees responsibility for the protection and conservation of property for beneficiaries who cannot share in the discharge of this responsibility and, therefore, are not associates in a joint enterprise for the conduct of business for profit" (emphasis added).[88]

    The APT is established by the execution of a written trust instrument, and title to property is conveyed to the trustees for the purpose of protecting and conserving it for the beneficiaries. The settlor-beneficiary stands in the same relation to the APT as he or she would if the trust were created by others for the settlor, and the beneficiaries, as such, do not participate in the discharge of the trustees' responsibility of protecting and conserving trust property.

    For these reasons, particularly in a common-law jurisdiction, the APT is classified as a trust.[89] As discussed above in section IV A 1 b iii (A), unexpected tax classification results may result where a "trust" is established in a civil law jurisdiction.[90]

In addressing this issue, the Internal Revenue Service has focused on whether the arrangement results in a separation of the beneficial enjoyment of trust assets from the responsibility for the management and conservation of such assets.[91]

(B) <u>Foreign or Domestic</u>

It may seem unusual to discuss whether a trust is a foreign or a domestic trust under the heading of "Offshore Trusts," but an offshore trust, as that term is used in this book,[92] may well be treated as a US trust for US income tax purposes. "Offshore Trust" is not a technical term. The correct technical term - for US income tax purposes - is "foreign trust."

Current tax law utilizes a two-pronged test to determine whether a trust is a US trust or a foreign trust for US income tax purposes.[93] A "foreign trust" is defined as a trust that does not qualify as a "United States person" under Internal Revenue Code § 7701(a)(30)(E). Section 7701(a)(30)(E) provides that a trust is a "United States person" if the trust meets *both* of the following requirements: (1) a court within the United States is able to exercise primary supervision over the administration of the trust (the so-called "court test"),[94] and (2) one or more United States persons have the authority to control all substantial decisions of the trust (the so-called "control test").[95] A trust that fails either of these requirements is a "foreign trust."

The term "offshore trust" is not a tax law term but rather is defined as above. An offshore trust can, if appropriate under the planning circumstances, be structured to be a US trust for US tax purposes. If the APT is to hold S-corporation stock it must qualify as a US grantor trust.[96]

ii. US income tax Consequences of Creation.

Internal Revenue Code § 684(a) requires a United States person who transfers appreciated property to a foreign trust to treat that transfer of property as a sale or exchange of such property for an amount equal to the fair market value of the property transferred, and thus recognize gain on the excess of the property's fair market value over its adjusted basis.[97] Section 684(b), however, provides that *this rule shall not apply* to a transfer by a United States person to a foreign trust *if* the foreign trust is a *grantor trust*.

Internal Revenue Code § 679 results in grantor trust treatment where a United States person is the settlor of a foreign trust with at least one US beneficiary. Thus, no gain will be recognized (nor income tax incurred) upon the establishment of a typical foreign asset protection trust.

iii. US income tax Consequences— Operation.

As stated in section IV A 2 b ii, above, in almost every case (if not in every case) the foreign trust will be treated as a grantor trust for US income tax purposes under § 679. If a trust is a grantor trust, US income tax law requires the grantor (settlor) of the trust to report the trust's income, deductions, and credits on the grantor's income tax return. In addition, transactions of any kind between the settlor and the trust will generate no income tax consequence whatsoever to the settlor or to the trust. Confusion among non-tax lawyers has resulted from the tax law requirement that the settlor report all of the trust's tax items on the settlor's personal income tax return, as this has been argued by plaintiff's counsel to indicate a retained income interest in or control over the trust. On several occasions we have been required to explain to litigation counsel that just because the tax law deems the settlor to be the "owner"[98] of the trust and requires the settlor to report all trust tax items on his/her income tax return -, whether distributed or not, that does not dictate the property and trust law consequences. One has nothing to do with the other.

It is beyond the scope of this book to discuss the grantor trust provisions in detail; however, the following is a generalized summary of the other provisions that may apply to an APT:

(A) §673 - Reversionary Interests. A trust will be a grantor trust if the grantor has a reversionary interest the value of which exceeds 5 percent of the trust assets at the inception of the trust.

(B) §674 - Power to Control Beneficial Enjoyment. A broadly applicable section, §674 will usually result in grantor trust status where any person has the power to add beneficiaries to the trust (other than only after-born or after-adopted children). For flexibility, and for asset protection purposes, an APT will often grant such a power to the trustees.

(C) §677 - Income for Benefit of the Grantor. Since one of the goals of asset protection planning is to preserve assets for one's own benefit during one's lifetime, the settlor and/or the settlor's spouse will almost always be designated as beneficiaries of the APT. Section 677 will result in grantor trust status when the trustee has the discretion (or is required) to distribute trust income to the settlor or the settlor's spouse.

iv. US estate/gift/GST tax Consequences.

Unless a reason exists for an alternate structure,[99] the APT will be structured so that transfers to it will constitute wholly incomplete gifts for purposes of federal gift tax rules (*i.e.*, no gift tax consequence).

Treasury Regulation § 25.2511-2(c) provides, *inter alia*, that a gift is incomplete (no gift) to the extent a reserved power gives the donor (settlor) the power to name new beneficiaries or to change the interests of the beneficiaries as between themselves, provided the power is not limited by an ascertainable standard.[100]

Thus, an APT provision reserving such an inter vivos or testamentary special power of appointment (or both)[101] to the settlor will result in transfers to the trust being incomplete gifts, with no attendant gift tax consequences, aside from the recommended filing an informational gift tax return.

A provision similar to the following should result in incomplete gift treatment.

> "During the lifetime of the Settlor, the Trustees shall distribute the Trust Fund or any part thereof to such one or more of the Settlor's issue [children, grandchildren, and so on], on such terms and conditions, and in such proportions, either outright or in trust, as the Settlor may from time to time appoint (direct the distribution of) by a written instrument executed by the Settlor and delivered to one or more of the Trustees, with such instrument specifically referring to and exercising this power of appointment."

Of course, distributions out of the trust to persons other than the settlor during the settlor's lifetime will constitute completed gifts.[102]

The other side of the "incomplete gift" coin is that the value of the APT will be included in the settlor's gross estate for US estate and generation skipping tax (GST) purposes.[103] Thus, the conventional estate tax planning considerations of utilizing the unified credit,[104] obtaining the marital deduction,[105] and the GST[106] must be addressed in the APT.

In order to address these issues, the APT should include all of the estate planning provisions typically included in a will or "living trust," including the credit shelter or bypass trust, the marital deduction trust or bequest, and provisions to effectively utilize the generation-skipping transfer tax exemption. It may be necessary to modify such provisions from standard usage to comport with the asset protection goal.[107] A detailed discussion of these requirements is beyond the scope of this book.

B. Trusts for Settlors Owning Community Property —Special Considerations[108]

As discussed above, if the APT is structured to render transfers to it as incomplete gifts, the value of the APT assets will be included in the settlor's gross estate for federal estate tax purposes upon his or her death. Under § 1014(a), the basis (cost) of property included in a decedent's estate is adjusted to its fair market value as of the date of the decedent's death (or alternate valuation date, if elected for estate tax purposes). The basis adjustment applies to most property included in a decedent's gross estate, including community and separate property. The extra advantage for the surviving spouse in a community property state arises from the fact that the basis of *all* of the community property is adjusted when the first spouse dies, even though only the decedent's one-half interest is included in his or her taxable estate.[109] This "double" basis adjustment for the survivor's interest in community property is a unique advantage that has no counterpart in common-law states.

Community assets held in a revocable trust receive the same double step-up in basis at death as any similar property acquired directly from a decedent. Because both halves of community property, not just the decedent's one-half interest, are eligible to receive a stepped-up basis on the first spouse's death, the planner must, *if possible under the circumstances,* avoid terminating the community property character of assets transferred to the APT. If the property loses its community property character, only the decedent's one-half interest will receive a new basis on death.

If the situs jurisdiction of the APT does not recognize the community nature of the property, then on the first spouse's death, the surviving spouse may not be entitled to a stepped-up basis on his or her share of the community trust assets under §1014(b)(6). In California, community property transferred to an irrevocable trust loses its community property character.

The Cook Islands has enacted legislation directed at the preservation of the double step-up for community property. Section 13J of the International Trusts Act 1984 provides that where a husband and wife transfer property to an international trust or to a trust that subsequently becomes an international trust (under Cook Islands law), and, immediately before being transferred, such property was community property, then the property will be deemed to continue as community property, and it will be dealt with under Cook Islands law according to the law of the jurisdiction establishing the community nature of the property.

In selecting a jurisdiction within which to settle an APT, for those settlors who reside in community property states, or who otherwise own community property, the Cook Islands may be the only jurisdiction in which the community property nature of the property may be preserved to qualify for the double basis adjustment at the first spouse's death.

C. Protective Trust Provisions

In this section, provisions that are typically thought of as "protective" of trust assets and/or income are discussed.

1. Discretionary Distribution Provision

a. Description.

A discretionary distribution provision vests the trustee with the decision regarding whether to distribute trust income and/or principal to a beneficiary. The discretion may be unfettered:

> "...the Trustees may, in their sole and absolute discretion, pay or apply the whole, any portion, or none of the net income of the Trust to, or in any manner the Trustees deem to be for the benefit of all, or any one or more of the Beneficiaries."

Or, the discretion may be limited by a broadly defined standard:

> "...the Trustees may, in their discretion, pay to or apply for the benefit of the Beneficiary, so much of the net income of his separate trust as the Trustees deem advisable to provide adequately and properly for the support, maintenance, health, medical care (including, but not limited to, dental, chiropractic, cosmetic surgical, and psychiatric care), welfare, education

(including, but not limited to, private schools [elementary, preparatory, junior high, and high school], tutoring, college, professional, vocational, language, artistic studies, and other post-graduate education), comfort, and emergency needs of the Beneficiary, and to enable the Beneficiary to maintain his/her accustomed standard of living, purchase a home, and/or invest in, purchase, or commence a business venture."

    b. <u>Effect.</u>

In short, the effect of a discretionary distribution provision is to limit the extent of the beneficiary's property interest in the trust. A maxim of asset protection planning is: "If you don't own it, it can't be taken from you." A property interest can be taken by a creditor. Where a trust contains a discretionary distribution provision, the property interest of a beneficiary only comes into existence when and to the extent the trustee decides to and makes a distribution to the beneficiary. A creditor of a beneficiary whose trust interest is subject to such a provision generally cannot reach the underlying trust assets, nor can the creditor compel the trustee to pay out income and/or principal (particularly not with an offshore trust). Thus, a discretionary distribution provision may provide a significant asset protection benefit.[110] This protection does not apply to situations where the trustee's discretion relates to the *time of payment,* such as where the beneficiary is ultimately to receive all of the trust income and/or principal.[111] Generally, a court (with jurisdiction over the trustee) will only interfere with a trustee's exercise or failure to exercise a discretionary distribution power when an abuse of discretion has been shown to have occurred.[112]

Trusts

2. Spendthrift Provision

   a. Description.

A spendthrift provision is a restraint on the voluntary or involuntary alienation (transfer or pledge) of a beneficiary's interest in a trust.

Although no specific language is required to create a spendthrift trust,[113] a sample provision in a trust instrument might read:

> "No Beneficiary shall have the right, power or authority to assign, transfer, dispose of, pledge, hypothecate, anticipate, encumber, or in any other manner alienate, impair, or create a charge upon the income, principal, or any other benefit devolving from all or any portion of any Trust created hereunder to which such Beneficiary may be entitled, and likewise, income or principal distributable, or which may become distributable to a Beneficiary, or any other benefit devolving on a Beneficiary with respect to any Trust hereunder shall not be subject to seizure, lien, levy, attachment, bankruptcy, transfer, assignment, garnishment, or any other legal process whatsoever, nor shall any such interest in income or principal or any other benefit hereunder be subject to interference or control by any creditor of any Beneficiary, nor subject to any claim for alimony or for the support of a spouse pursuant to a decree of separate maintenance or separation agreement, until distribution is actually made to such Beneficiary; and to the extent permitted by Applicable

Law, the Trust Funds administered hereunder, until actually paid over and distributed to one or more Beneficiaries, as herein provided, shall be held by the Trustees free and clear of all manner of anticipation or voluntary or involuntary alienation."

A provision converting required trust distributions into discretionary distributions upon the occurrence of certain creditor related events has been held to be a spendthrift provision.[114] An example of such a provision would be:

"In addition to the foregoing, no distribution of Trust income and/or principal otherwise required to be made under any provision of this Settlement shall be made to any Beneficiary hereunder if, at the time such nondiscretionary distribution is to be made, such Beneficiary: is insolvent (where the Trustees determine, in their sole discretion, that the Beneficiary's insolvency would prevent the Beneficiary from personally enjoying the distribution), has filed a petition in bankruptcy (where the bankruptcy proceeding is ongoing), or otherwise would not personally enjoy the income or principal to be distributed. In connection with the preceding sentence, the Trustees, in their sole discretion, may or may not inquire into the Beneficiary's solvency, bankruptcy status, and/or the likelihood that the Beneficiary will personally enjoy the intended distribution (and the Trustees shall incur no liability whatsoever for failing to so inquire, or for doing so in an inadequate, incomplete, or incompetent manner), and the Trustees may accept as sufficient proof, or reject, any oral or written statement of the Beneficiary in regard to the matters mentioned in the preceding sentence. During the period in which required distributions are suspended by reason of this provision, the Trustees may, in their sole discretion, make such discretionary distributions of income and/or principal to or for the benefit of the affected Beneficiary, as the Trustees deem advisable to provide adequately and properly for the support, maintenance, health, medical care (including, but not limited to, dental, chiropractic, cosmetic surgical, and psychiatric care), welfare, education (including, but not limited to, private schools [elementary, preparatory, junior high, and high school], tutoring, college, professional, vocational, language, artistic studies, and other post-graduate education), comfort, and emergency needs of the Beneficiary, and to enable the Beneficiary to maintain his/her accustomed standard of living."

Similarly, provisions effecting a forfeiture of a beneficiary's trust interest upon an attempt by the beneficiary to transfer it, or by his creditors to reach it, is a type of spendthrift provision, albeit somewhat Draconian. An example provided by the Restatement of Trusts illustrates this.

"A transfers property to B in trust to pay the income to C for life and to pay the principal on C's death to

D. By the terms of the trust, it is provided that if C should convey his interest, or if his creditors should attempt to reach it, or if he should become bankrupt, his interest under the trust should cease, and the income should be paid to C's wife during the remainder of C's life. C becomes bankrupt. His interest under the trust terminates."[115]

b. <u>Effect.</u>

Depending upon the relationship to the trust of the beneficiary and the creditor, the spendthrift provision may provide a significant asset protection benefit for the trust beneficiary.[116]

3. <u>Duress Provision</u>

a. <u>Background/description.</u>

The trustee of a trust administers the trust. "Administers the trust" means that, in general, the trustee invests trust assets, distributes trust income and/or assets to the beneficiaries in accordance with the terms of the trust, and makes all decisions regarding trust assets. An important fact to understand about trusts is that the trust instrument can be created with very flexible provisions. Therefore, even though a trustee *normally* invests trust assets, distributes trust income and/or assets, and makes all decisions regarding the trust, a trust instrument may empower a person or persons other than the trustee to advise the trustee, and/or to direct or veto an act or decision of the trustee, and/or a trust instrument may grant a non-trustee the power to remove and replace a trustee with or without cause, and/or a trust instrument may grant a non-trustee the power to direct the distribution of trust income and/or assets (a power of appointment). *Even in those situations where a trust instrument empowers a non-trustee, as in the examples in the preceding sentence, it is **always** the trustee who carries out the exercise of those powers.* Therefore, the typical duress clause will direct the trustee to ignore any such advice, order, or instruction where it is given "under duress" (as that term is defined in the trust instrument) by the person holding such power(s) under the instrument. A properly drafted duress provision will include a *mechanism*[117] by which the trustee (who carries out the exercise of a power by another) can be 100 percent certain that no duress is involved. An example of a duress provision would be:

> "The Settlor directs that this Settlement be administered consistent with its terms, free of judicial intervention and without order, approval, or other action of any court. To the extent any person is granted the power hereunder to do any act or to compel any act on the part of one or more of the Trustees, or has the authority to render advice to one or more of the Trustees, or to otherwise approve, compel, or veto any action or exercise any power which affects or will affect this Settlement, each Trustee is directed, to the extent the respective Trustee then in office would not be subject to personal liability or personal exposure (for example, by being held in contempt of court or other such sanction by a court having jurisdiction over the respective Trustee): (1) to accept or recognize only instructions or advice, or the effects of any approval, veto, or compelled action or the exercise of any power, which are

given by or are the result of persons acting of their own free will and not under compulsion of any legal process or like authority; and (2) to ignore any advice or any directive, veto, order, or like decree, or the results or effects thereof, of any court, administrative body, or any tribunal whatsoever, or of past or present Trustees, of any Protector hereunder, or of any other person, where: (a) such has been instigated by directive, order, or like decree of any court, administrative body, or other tribunal, or (b) the person attempting to compel the act, or attempting to exercise the authority to render advice, or otherwise attempting to compel or veto any action or exercise any power that affects or will affect this Settlement, is not a person either appointed or so authorized or the like, pursuant to the terms and conditions of this Settlement. For purposes of this Settlement, a person shall be deemed to be acting under compulsion, and otherwise involuntarily, during any period of Adjudicated Incapacity [also defined in the trust instrument] of said person."

    b. <u>Effect.</u>

Since these provisions are typically utilized in offshore trusts, where the trustee is located in a jurisdiction other than the jurisdiction of the person holding the various powers subject to negation by the clause, the duress provision can have the effect of permitting the retention or granting of significant control over the trust, by or to non-trustees, such as the settlor (*not recommended*) or other persons, while at the same time precluding the forced exercise of such powers.[118]

A US court could order the US power holder to exercise the power in a manner that will benefit a creditor, but such an order would constitute duress under a properly drafted provision, an order given under which must be ignored by the trustee (over whom the US court does *not* have jurisdiction). It has been suggested that, in a circumstance as has been described in the preceding sentence, the US court could hold the power holder in contempt (incarcerating him or her) until that person found a means to force the trustee to violate the provisions of the trust (and be subject to exposure from other trust beneficiaries under the laws of the foreign jurisdiction). The US Supreme Court has held that inability to comply with a court order is a complete defense to a contempt charge (*See* IV A 1 b vi, above).[119]

4. Flight Provision

a. Description.

A flight provision (variously called a "fleeing clause" or "Cuba clause") empowers the trustee (or a trust protector - see below), in furtherance of the prime objective of preservation of the trust, to change the situs (location) of trust administration, trustee, governing law, and to transfer trust assets to effect such changes. Such a provision is commonly included in an offshore trust to address various situations, including civil unrest (in the days before asset protection), or an unfavorable change in the law or political climate of the situs jurisdiction. An example of a flight provision:

"The Trustees may, by a written declaration executed by them, at any time or times and from time to time during the Trust Period, as they deem advisable in their discretion for the benefit or security of this Trust Fund or any portion hereof, remove (or decline to remove) all or part of the assets and/or the situs of administration thereof from one jurisdiction to another jurisdiction and/or declare that this Settlement shall from the date of such declaration take effect in accordance with the law of some other state or territory in any part of the World and thereupon the courts of such other jurisdiction shall have the power to effectuate the purposes of this Settlement to such extent. In no event, however, shall the law of some other state or territory be any place under the law of which: (1) substantially all of the powers and provisions herein declared and contained would not be enforceable or capable of being exercised and so taking effect; or (2) this Settlement would not be irrevocable. From the date of such declaration the law of the state or territory named therein shall be the Applicable Law, but subject always to the power conferred by this Section ___ of this ARTICLE ___ and until any further declaration be made hereunder. So often as any such declaration as aforesaid shall be made, the Trustees shall be at liberty to make such consequential alterations or additions in or to the powers, discretions and provisions of this Settlement as the Trustees may consider necessary or desirable to ensure that the provisions of this Settlement shall, *mutatis mutandis*, be so valid and effective as they are under the Applicable Law governing this Settlement at the time the power contained herein is exercised. The determination of the Trustees as to any such removal or change in Applicable Law shall be conclusive and binding on all persons interested or claiming to be interested in this Settlement, and the written declaration executed by the Trustees from time to time effecting any such change in situs or Applicable Law is hereby deemed to be a term or provision of this Settlement as if included herein on the date of execution of this Settlement by the Settlor."

    b. <u>Effect.</u>

The flight clause, *if coupled with a mechanism to insure that it will be effective*,[120] provides a substantial safety net for a trust in the event of an unfavorable change in the law of the situs jurisdiction, civil unrest or political change in the situs jurisdiction, *or in the event of an anticipated attack on the trust in the situs jurisdiction by a creditor*. Such a provision would permit a trust to change its situs, trustee, governing law, and the courts in which litigation concerning it must be brought - an important asset protection tool in the face of an oncoming creditor challenge against the trust in the offshore jurisdiction.

The laws of several foreign jurisdictions specifically recognize the validity, and anticipate the use of the flight clause. Section 5-(1) of the Trusts (Choice of Governing Law) Act, 1989 (The Bahamas), provides a typical example:

"5-(1) Where a term of a trust so provides, the governing law may be changed to or from the laws of The Bahamas if -

(a) in the case of a change to the laws of The Bahamas, such change is recognised by the governing law previously in effect; and

(b) in the case of a change from the laws of The Bahamas, the new governing law would recognise the validity of the trust and the respective interests of the beneficiaries.[121]

5. <u>Trust Protector Provision</u>

a. <u>Description.</u>

The trust protector provision, commonly found in offshore trusts, may be compared to an "of counsel" designation of an attorney on a law firm's letterhead. That is, it means whatever the trust instrument says that it means.

The trust protector (or, in some cases, the committee of trust protectors) is not a trustee but will have certain powers over the trust. Where the trust protector is located in the United States, any powers granted to the trust protector under the trust instrument should be constructed to be veto powers, and not powers to direct the trustee to take an action.

A typical trust protector veto power provision might read:

> "Notwithstanding anything to the contrary contained herein, and in particular, notwithstanding anything conferring an absolute or uncontrolled discretion on the Trustees hereof, each and every power and discretion vested in the Trustees by such provisions of this

Settlement as are specified in Schedule ___ attached hereto and incorporated herein by this reference shall only be exercisable by them, subject always to the power of the Protector to veto any exercise by the Trustees of such power or discretion, and accordingly, the Trustees shall be required to provide the Protector with sufficient prior notice of their intent to exercise any such powers or discretions to permit the Protector reasonable advance opportunity within which to consider the factors relevant to the Protector's determination to veto or refrain from vetoing the exercise of the power or discretion. The Protector's exercise or nonexercise of this veto power shall be communicated in writing to the Trustees and failure to so communicate in a timely fashion provided notice is actually received by the Protector shall be treated by the Trustees as a veto of the proposed exercise of the power or discretion; provided, however, if one or more of the Trustees reasonably believes that failure by the Protector to so communicate is due to the Protector being restrained or enjoined from doing so, then such failure to communicate shall be deemed to be an acquiescence by the Protector. It is further provided that, notwithstanding anything to the contrary otherwise herein expressed or implied, no discretion or power conferred upon the Protector, or upon any other person by this Settlement, or by any rule of law, or arising in consequence of the exercise of any power conferred upon the Protector, or any other person by this Settlement, shall be exercised, and nothing contained herein shall operate, so as to cause the Protector to be successful in ordering or vetoing any action or causing any result which is not of the Protector's own free will, or which is otherwise the result of the Protector acting under the duress or influence of an outside force. In order to implement the foregoing veto power, the Protector may at any time, or from time to time, require the establishment of (and the transfer of the Trust Estate to) Trust bank and/or brokerage accounts, and/or other forms of ownership under which both the Protector's signature and the signature of one or more of the Trustees (as specified by the Protector) would be required to effect any transfer or conveyance."

b. Effect

Properly structured, *with an independent protector*, the protector provision enables oversight and enhanced protection of the trust. The provision enables the trust protector to exercise significant negative controls over any specified aspect of the trust, even, as shown in the last sentence of the above provision, a direct veto power over the transfer of funds, securities, and other assets by requiring both the trustee's and the protector's signatures <u>at the financial institution level</u> to effect a transfer of funds out of an account - *a very significant security feature*. In addition to the veto power set forth above, the trust instrument may grant other specific powers to the protector, such as a power to remove and replace a trustee with or without cause (subject, of course, to the duress provision discussed above). As with provisions appointing trustees, the trust protector provision should include language addressing succession and related issues. To maximize the efficacy of the protector provision, the authors recommend utilizing a professional protector company whose job it is to deal with such trust matters on a daily basis. In the author's experience, utilizing a friend or relative as the trust protector can be problematic. What if, several years after the trust is established, the protector is no longer a friend? What if the protector is on vacation when urgent protector action is needed?

The concept and use of the trust protector provision is recognized by the laws of several foreign jurisdictions. A well-drafted example of such a statute is found in §16, Trusts Act 1992 (Belize), which provides

"16. (1) The terms of a trust may provide for the office of protector of the trust.

(2) The protector shall have the following powers:

(a) (unless the terms of the trust shall otherwise provide) the power to remove a trustee and to appoint a new or additional trustee;

(b) such further powers as are conferred on the protector by the terms of the trust or of this Act.

(3) The protector of a trust may also be a settlor, a trustee or a beneficiary of the trust.

(4) In the exercise of his office, the protector shall not be accounted or regarded as a trustee.

(5) Subject to the terms of the trust, in the exercise of his office a protector shall owe a fiduciary duty to the beneficiaries of the trust or to the purpose for which the trust is created.

(6) Where there is more than one protector of a trust then, subject to the terms of the trust, any functions conferred on the

protectors may be exercised if more than one half of the protectors for the time being agree on its exercise.

(7) A protector who dissents from a decision of the majority of protectors may require his dissent to be recorded in writing."[122]

6. Other Protective Provisions

Other provisions that tend to enhance the protective aspects of a trust include:

a. Extension provision.

This is a provision granting the trustees the discretion to extend the trust term. Such a provision would prove particularly useful in a situation where a trust was about to terminate and distribute assets to a beneficiary who was then battling with a creditor or otherwise faced with a significant liability.

b. Principal and income allocation provision.

This provision grants the trustee the discretion to allocate receipts and disbursements between principal and income in the manner deemed best by the trustee.

Ordinarily thought of as a means to provide flexibility, such a provision could prove useful in a situation when, for example, all trust income is required to be distributed to a beneficiary with significant creditor problems. In the exercise of its discretion, the trustee could allocate all receipts to trust principal, thereby leaving no income "required to be distributed." Of course, in the case of a domestic trustee, a complaining creditor could always allege an abuse of discretion by the trustee, and if successful, cause a distribution to the beneficiary that could be reached by the creditor.

c. Revision of beneficial interests.

Such a provision would grant the trustee the discretion to revise the beneficial interests of a beneficiary, even to the extent of excluding such person as a beneficiary and adding other persons as trust beneficiaries. Such a provision would essentially have the same effect as a discretionary distribution provision, with the possible additional effect of being effective in a domestic trust.

d. Custodian trustee provision.

Where permitted by law, a trust (usually an offshore trust) may be settled in one jurisdiction under the administration of a managing trustee. A provision in the trust instrument would authorize the appointment of a trustee in another jurisdiction as the "custodian trustee." Title to trust assets would be held in the name of the custodian trustee, but any litigation involving the trust would be required to be brought in the jurisdiction where the managing trustee is resident, and under which laws the trust is then governed. The trust instrument could further provide that, upon the filing of any litigation against the trust in the managing trustee's jurisdiction, the managing trustee is deemed removed as trustee, with the managing trustee position devolving upon the custodian trustee (or the same could be set forth in a letter of wishes). Such a provision would have the effect of requiring the aggressive creditor to bring his action at least twice in offshore jurisdictions with separate lawyers and under separate legal systems.

For example, a trust could be established in The Bahamas, utilizing a Bahamian trust company as the managing trustee, and a Cook Islands trust company (halfway around the world) as the custodian (title holding) trustee. The governing law would be the law of The

Bahamas, and the appropriate forum for bringing an action against the trust would be in The Bahamian courts. After a creditor has gone through the time and expense of engaging Bahamian counsel and filing his suit in The Bahamas, he will find (1) that The Bahamian trust company is no longer the trustee, and (2) that he must start his litigation all over again on the other side of the world with new Cook Islands counsel in the Cook Islands courts.[123]

Such an automatic provision may prove more efficient than a flight clause in daunting a creditor, at the cost of dual trustee fees, however.

D. Offshore Asset Protection Strategies.

Offshore strategies typically include the use of offshore trusts and other entities. The mere mention of offshore planning will often raise concerns (some justified), among which are security of assets and tax issues. Careful due diligence is the best way to address these concerns. How do you do this? Make certain you are obtaining advice from or working with a recognized expert **lawyer** in the field - not just someone with a flashy website (see XI, below, on how to select an asset protection attorney). Reputable lawyers can be checked out through the state bar where the lawyer is licensed. This can be analogized as getting proper medical advice. While you cannot be expected to learn how to perform a complex surgical procedure, the best chance for success in implementing that procedure is to seek out the surgeon who specializes in the field, who performs that procedure every day, and who is recognized as an expert by his peers.

In considering asset protection planning strategies, we need to distinguish between two major asset groups: liquid assets (cash and publicly traded securities) and immovable assets (such as real estate, equipment, etc.). Different asset protection strategies must be used to protect the assets in each of those two groups.

1. Cash and Publicly Traded Securities (liquid assets)

Effectively protecting liquid assets involves having the trustee of the offshore trust open a financial account for the trust at an offshore financial institution. Such an institution would typically be a bank in Liechtenstein or Switzerland (like you, your client's trust can open an account anywhere in the world, and clients seem to prefer Switzerland and/or Liechtenstein because of their long history of financial security). What kind of assets can be held in this account? The account could be comprised of cash held in any currency (including US dollars), publicly traded securities (including US publicly traded securities and US treasury securities if desired), and foreign securities (depending upon investment strategy). You might ask, "Why can't my client just open a Swiss account without the trust?" Here's why. Our laws require the client to report[124] that account in annual tax return filings. If someone gets a judgment against your client, that judgment creditor will be able to see those tax returns, find out about the Swiss account, and ask the court to simply order your client to cash in the Swiss account to pay the judgment. Although your client also has to report[125] the offshore account held in his/her trust, a <u>properly structured</u> offshore trust is different. The offshore trustee company (not located in the United States) controls the trust (not your client) and the US court cannot order that trustee company to do anything. Translation: your client's assets are unreachable by the US court system, and that = protection. Repeating what was said in IV 1 b iv, above: What type of criteria should we consider in selecting an offshore financial institution for asset protection purposes? In addition to customary factors such as financial condition, stability, and local banking laws, the offshore financial institution must not have any US branch, because if the offshore financial institution did have a US branch, a US court could exert some type of pressure or influence on that US branch to the detriment of your protective structure.

2. Immovable Assets: Real Estate, Equipment, LLC Member Interests, Etc.

Effectively protecting assets like real estate, LLC member interests, and equipment (immovable assets) requires the implementation of an *ancillary strategy* together with the offshore trust. The belief that real estate (for example) can be effectively protected by enclosing it in a metaphorical box called a limited liability company, limited partnership, or corporation does not take into account the very real likelihood that a "result-oriented" judge (recall that you did not think your client would be treated fairly by the US legal system) will disregard the entity and go directly after the real estate. The only effective method available to protect an immovable asset is to make the asset unattractive to a creditor by removing its value – – *make the asset not worth going after.* Think about it. Would you spend your time and money to sue someone if all they had was a piece of real property worth $1 million encumbered by a $950,000 mortgage? This technique is implemented by pledging the asset as collateral for a loan (from a lender **unrelated to your client**) and by then protecting the loan proceeds with your client's other liquid assets in your client's offshore trust. The loan proceeds can then be invested safely, protected inside your client's trust, in interest-earning investments, significantly reducing the net annual interest cost of this approach.

Some offshore trust companies have relationships with lenders who are willing to assist with this type of planning.

3. Entity Trusts

Although one might not ordinarily think of an entity (a corporation, partnership, LLC, or a trust) as creating its own trust, entities create trusts all the time. For example, pension trusts, profit-sharing trusts, and non-qualified deferred compensation trusts are commonly created by entities. So why not asset protection trusts as well?

An entity trust would be appropriate, for example, to protect assets of an entity in a high-risk business. Such a trust could be used to safeguard the entity's excess cash and/or to hold the proceeds of an equity stripping loan transaction used to protect the entity's immovable assets. See above discussion regarding immovable assets.

The entity trust provides two-pronged protection: first, it provides protection for the entity itself from potential future creditors of the entity, and second, it provides protection for the owner(s) of the entity from his/her creditors with respect to the ownership interest(s) in the entity. It accomplishes the latter by *removing the internal value* of the entity to the extent assets are held in the entity trust. With the internal value of the entity removed, the entity ownership interest itself becomes a far less attractive asset to the creditors of the owner(s), because the availability of entity assets (equity) for litigation settlement has been reduced or removed.

For example, a CPA partnership with twenty partners had accumulated significant liquid assets to fund the retirement of its partners. The partners recognized the high risk of litigation inherent in the accounting profession. For a variety of reasons, the partners decided not to make current distributions of the liquid assets but rather have decided that the partnership will form an offshore asset protection (entity) trust. The trust will then be funded with partnership liquid assets not required for current operations (i.e., the accumulated retirement funds). Upon a partner's retirement, a retirement distribution might be made from the entity trust to the partner or, if the retiring partner was being sued at that time, the distribution could be made directly to an offshore trust previously created by the retiring partner, thereby completely eliminating any possible exposure of that distribution to the partner's judgment creditor.

4. Combination Structures

The offshore trust is sometimes implemented in combination with other entities, such as limited partnerships and/or limited liability companies (we'll refer to such an entity here as a "holding company"). In such a structure, the offshore trust will own a majority (sometimes 100 percent in an LLC) interest in the holding company. Your client may manage the holding company on a day-to-day basis, retaining complete control of and signature authority over the assets and accounts held in the holding company. Such a structure has its drawbacks, however. First, if it is to be used, it should only be used when no potential threat of litigation is on the horizon. Second, if it is used, and a serious litigation threat arises, it will be necessary to "pull the plug" on the holding company - that is, to liquidate it into the offshore trust (its owner). If it does become necessary to pull the plug, additional legal and trustee fees will be incurred in liquidating the holding company and arranging for the trust to open financial accounts to receive the liquid assets from the holding company. Some offshore financial institutions may refuse to accept an account (even though the account would be in the name of the trust) where the settlor of the trust is being sued - your client might get caught between a rock and a hard place. This latter problem may be avoided if an offshore account is also opened directly in the trust at its inception - before a problem arises.

5. Group Trusts

This technique was developed to make effective asset protection planning available to a broader spectrum of clients: those who are unwilling or unable to pay for individualized offshore trust planning. The fees and costs involved in group trust planning are approximately 40 percent less than those associated with individualized offshore planning, yet *the protection is the same as individualized offshore trust planning*. A group trust is created by a single trust instrument. It will have a minimum of four settlors ("participants"; it is anticipated that the participants will know each other), with married couples being treated as one settlor (for this purpose only). Each settlor will have a separate **subtrust** under the instrument, and one settlor being sued will have no effect on any other settlor. No additional settlors can be added after the inception of the trust.

Where is group trust planning typically appropriate? For example, by a group of physicians who practice together, members of a church group who want to safely invest their personal funds together, and similar homogeneous groups.

Although liquid assets, such as publicly traded securities, can be commingled in a single offshore financial account within the trust, separate accounting to each settlor and strict confidentiality of financial matters between settlors is maintained. Thus, for example, if a settlor contributes IBM shares to his subtrust, any dividends on those shares would be allocated solely to that settlor's subtrust, and any gains or losses generated from the sale of that security would likewise be allocated only to that settlor's subtrust. To avoid the accounting burden associated with maintaining such a single account, separate accounts can be opened for each subtrust. Real estate and other immovable assets can also be effectively protected for each settlor through the implementation of an ancillary loan structure (equity stripping).

The dispositive provisions (how trust assets are distributed during a settlor's lifetime and on a settlor's death) are standardized within the trust, meaning the provisions would be the same for each settlor. Thus, if one settlor had a child with special needs or otherwise required specialized dispositive provisions, the group trust would not be appropriate for that person.

6. Enhanced IRA Protection

IRA assets are protected to varying degrees by each of the states and under the federal bankruptcy law. In order to secure 100 percent protection from all creditors for IRA assets (and not be concerned whether a court will respect the state-law provided IRA protection), your client must implement an IRA enhancement strategy. Following the asset protection rule of "removing the ability of any US court to disrupt your client's planning," enhanced protection of IRA assets can be accomplished by causing the IRA to establish a single member offshore limited liability company governed by *properly structured* documents containing special protective provisions. The IRA contributes (transfers) all of its assets to its LLC in exchange for a 100 percent ownership interest (member interest) in the LLC, leaving the IRA custodian (in the United States) directly holding only a member interest in the offshore LLC (a specialized US IRA custodian is required to implement this planning - one who is able to permit "self-directed" IRAs). The LLC is managed by an independent offshore management company. The investment assets would be held in a suitable offshore financial institution (see discussion above for criteria to be considered in selecting an offshore financial institution).

At this point, the retirement plan assets are held at an offshore financial institution, but they remain invested in the same securities and managed by the same investment advisor (even a US advisor) as they were before. Couldn't a US court force the LLC owner (the IRA custodian) to turn over the LLC assets? No, because under the carefully drafted specialized provisions of the governing documents, the offshore LLC manager (who is in control of the assets) is only permitted to act when the LLC owner (the IRA custodian) is giving directions <u>voluntarily</u> - without any US court interference. In this structure, the IRA assets are beyond the reach of any US court and are thus absolutely protected.

E. What Should a Personal Asset Protection Trust Include at a Minimum?

A personal asset protection trust should include "core" estate planning provisions. By this, we mean it should include language disposing of your client's assets upon his/her death to his/her heirs. It should also include and take into account US estate tax planning. That discussion and those provisions are beyond the scope of this book.

CHAPTER V

FRAUDULENT TRANSFERS/ CONVEYANCES—VOIDABLE TRANSACTIONS

It is important to understand that in nearly every instance, a creditor's attack on a properly structured asset protection plan will be based upon a fraudulent transfer allegation. Thus, it is crucial to have a basic understanding of your state's Fraudulent Transfer/ Fraudulent Conveyance Act. This section V encompasses a discussion of fraudulent transfer issues related to the planning structures discussed herein. Unless specified to the contrary, the term "fraudulent transfer" will include the term "fraudulent conveyance," although the Uniform Fraudulent Conveyance Act is not separately discussed herein, since much of that Act survives today in the Uniform Fraudulent Transfer Act ("UFTA"). Substantial misunderstanding surrounds fraudulent transfer law. This stems from the root word, "fraud," contained in the term "fraudulent transfer" and from the frequent (and erroneous) shorthand use of the term "fraud" when the term "fraudulent transfer" is intended. *It is thus critical for the planner to distinguish between "fraud" and "fraudulent transfers," as they are two entirely different things.* Black's Law Dictionary defines fraud as follows:

Fraudulent Transfers/Conveyances—Voidable Transactions

1. A knowing misrepresentation of the truth or concealment of a material fact to induce another to act to his or her detriment. Fraud is usu. a tort, but in some cases (esp. when the conduct is willful) it may be a crime. 2. A misrepresentation made recklessly without belief in its truth to induce another person to act. 3. A tort arising from a knowing misrepresentation, concealment of material fact, or reckless misrepresentation made to induce another to act to his or her detriment.

This can be seen as ***entirely different from* Black's *definition of fraudulent conveyance (transfer)*.**

A transfer of property for little or no consideration, made for the purpose of hindering or delaying a creditor by putting the property beyond the creditor's reach; a transaction by which the owner of real or personal property seeks to place the property beyond the reach of creditors.

As a result of the continuous confusion and misunderstanding of these terms, the Uniform Law Commission unanimously adopted (in mid-July 2014) the Uniform Voidable Transactions Act ("UVTA"). The UVTA is intended to replace the UFTA, and the major change is in the title of the new act. Nothing of substance was changed in the UVTA, the new title being adopted to alleviate the above-discussed confusion and to clearly describe the effect of a court finding a "voidable transaction." A side effect is to eliminate the very negative connotation of the word fraudulent in the UFTA.

A. General

Fraudulent transfer law in the United States has evolved from the Statute of Elizabeth, enacted in England in 1571,[126] and is currently found in §548 of the Bankruptcy Code,[127] and in the fraudulent transfer statutes of the states.

1. Definition

In general in the United States, a transfer made by a debtor is a fraudulent transfer as to a creditor whose claim arose before *or after* the transfer was made, if the debtor made the transfer with *actual intent* to hinder, delay, or defraud [meaning: defeat the claim of] <u>any</u> creditor of the debtor.[128] A transfer is also a fraudulent transfer, *regardless of the debtor's intent*, where it is made without receiving a reasonably equivalent value in exchange, *and* the debtor was engaged or about to engage in a business or a transaction for which the debtor's remaining assets were unreasonably small in relation to the business or transaction, or the debtor intended to incur, or should have reasonably known he or she would incur, debts beyond his or her ability to pay them as they became due.[129] The Bankruptcy Code contains similar provisions.[130]

A transfer is automatically a fraudulent transfer as to a creditor whose claim arose before the transfer, where the transfer was made without receiving a reasonably equivalent value in the exchange, *and* the debtor was insolvent at the time or was rendered insolvent as a result of the transfer.[131]

Section 2 of the UFTA provides that a debtor is insolvent if the sum of the debtor's debts exceeds the fair market value of the debtor's assets. In addition, a debtor who is not paying his or her debts as they become due is presumed to be insolvent.[132]

Section 1(2) of the UFTA defines "asset," for purposes of the Act, to include all property of the debtor,[133] *except* property to the extent it is encumbered by a valid lien (the amount of the lien is also not counted), property to the extent it is generally exempt under non-bankruptcy law [meaning any non-bankruptcy federal and state law creditor exemptions], and an interest in property held in tenancy by the entireties to the extent such interest is not reachable [under that state's law] by a creditor holding a claim against only one spouse. In addition, for purposes of section 2 of the UFTA, the term "asset" does not include any value that can only be realized by setting aside the debtor's fraudulent transfers.[134] A "debt" is defined for UFTA purposes as a liability on a claim.[135] A "claim" is broadly defined to include any right to a payment, "whether or not the right is reduced to judgment, liquidated, unliquidated, fixed, contingent, matured, unmatured, disputed, undisputed, legal, equitable, secured, or unsecured."[136]

Thus, liabilities that may not be reflected on a debtor's balance sheet, such as a shareholder's personal guarantee of a corporate debt, lease obligations, PBGC claims, taxes, environmental claims, and the like, would be included as debts in a solvency analysis.[137] Finally, "debts" do not include debts to the extent secured by liens on property that is not included as an asset.[138]

Example: State X entirely exempts the homestead property of an individual from the claims of creditors. A has the following assets and debts:

Bank accounts:	50,000
Homestead (value):	100,000
Mortgage on homestead:	<75,000>
Other debts:	50,000

Based upon these figures, a transfer by A of one dollar would be a fraudulent transfer, because A would be rendered insolvent by the transfer of one dollar. Why? Because only the bank accounts and the other debts are taken into account, and if A transferred one dollar, he would have reduced the value of his assets below the amount of his countable liabilities, rendering him insolvent.[139]

    a. The transfer.

Although seemingly self-evident, in order for the fraudulent transfer rules to apply, a transfer must have taken place. Section 1(12) of the UFTA defines "transfer" as "every mode, direct or indirect, absolute or conditional, voluntary or involuntary, of disposing of or parting with an *asset* or an interest in an asset, and includes payment of money, release, lease, and creation of a lien or other encumbrance."

As mentioned above, section 1(2) of the UFTA excludes from the definition of "asset" for purposes of the Act property exempt under non-bankruptcy law, an interest in property held as tenants by the entireties, to the extent such interest is not reachable by a creditor holding a claim against only one spouse, and property to the extent it is encumbered by a valid lien.

> Example: Dr. X lives in state Y, whose laws exempt tenancy by the entireties property from the claims of a creditor of one of the spouses. In 2004, Dr. X attended a seminar at which he learned of the creditor protection facility of tenancy by the entireties property. After the seminar, Dr. X and his wife conveyed all of their then-existing assets into tenancy by the entireties

Fraudulent Transfers/Conveyances—Voidable Transactions

ownership, and took title to subsequently acquired property in this manner.

As of the beginning of 2014, the net value of Dr. and Mrs. X's tenancy by the entireties assets totaled $3 million. In June, 2014, Dr. X was named as a defendant in a malpractice action wherein damages in the amount of $5 million are being sought.

In July 2014, Mrs. X is diagnosed with a terminal illness and Dr. X consults a **qualified** asset protection lawyer to determine what can be done regarding the potential loss of all of the tenancy by the entireties properties in the event the creditor were successful, and Mrs. X dies (*remember*, the protection afforded by the tenancy by the entireties vanishes instantly upon the death of Mrs. X).

Being familiar with the fraudulent transfer statutes of state Y, which are identical to the UFTA, the lawyer advises Dr. X that he and Mrs. X may transfer their tenancy by the entireties assets into a structure that will provide continued protection in the event of Mrs. X's death, because tenancy by the entireties assets do not constitute "assets" under state Y's UFTA. Since such properties do not constitute assets under the statute, their conveyance into a protective structure cannot, by law, constitute a "transfer"; and thus, a conveyance of such properties into a protective structure that will afford creditor protection in the event of Mrs. X's death, will not [*cannot*] constitute a fraudulent transfer.[140]

Properties excluded from the definition of "asset" under the UFTA may not be taken into account for any purpose of the UFTA, including for purposes of determining a debtor's solvency.

b. Which creditors are protected?.

Section 4(a) of the UFTA protects a creditor whose "claim arose *before or after* the transfer was made." A literal interpretation of this clause might lead one to conclude that a transfer that satisfies the intent or equivalent value criteria of the statute could be attacked by any creditor, regardless of how long after the transfer the creditor's claim arose.[141] Fortunately, for asset protection purposes, this is not how the courts have interpreted such statutes.

Although the fraudulent transfer laws vary among the jurisdictions, it appears that a class of creditors, sometimes referred to as "future potential creditors" or "possible future creditors" remain unprotected by such laws.

In *Hurlbert v. Shackleton*,[142] Dr. Shackleton had been notified in 1983 that his malpractice insurance would be canceled in January 1984. Almost immediately following receipt of the notice of cancellation, Dr. Shackleton made numerous transfers of property because he couldn't "get malpractice insurance, and...wanted to cover all the bases."

Subsequent to the transfers in issue, Dr. Shackleton committed an act of malpractice on Hurlbert. Hurlbert sued and obtained a judgment and sought to set aside (undo), among others, a transfer into a tenancy by the entireties form of ownership made by Dr. Shackleton *prior* to the act of malpractice upon which the judgment was based.

The trial court found in favor of Dr. Shackleton, drawing a distinction between "probable" and "possible" future creditors and holding the latter category to be unprotected by the statute.

In the appellate decision,[143] the court found that such a distinction was not relevant, but that where a creditor was not in existence at the time of a transfer, the creditor had the burden of proving that the debtor harbored the actual intent to defraud the subsequent creditor.

In *Oberst v. Oberst*,[144] the court, in addressing the future creditor issue, made a distinction between transfers intended to place assets beyond the reach of a particular creditor or series of creditors - which would be fraudulent transfers, and transfers made by a debtor who is merely looking to his future well-being - which would be permissible.

In *Klein v. Klein*,[145] Mr. Klein, a police officer, petitioned the court of equity to partition realty, the title to which had been taken in Mrs. Klein's name alone, based upon her oral agreement to convey the property to the two of them upon Mr. Klein's retirement. Title to the property had been taken in Mrs. Klein's name alone at a time when no creditor of Mr. Klein existed, with the *stated purpose of protecting the property* from the possibility that Mr. Klein might be sued for false arrest or for some other act that he might commit in connection with the performance of his duties as a police officer.

The court noted that equity would not compel the action sought by Mr. Klein if the original transfer (titling the property in Mrs. Klein's name alone) had been made with the intent to hinder and delay creditors. In holding for Mr. Klein, the court stated:

"... there has been found no authority that an action such as this must fail for the reason that the grantor, who was without creditors, feared for future dangers, real or imaginative. Surely his hands were as clean as anyone who ever came into equity. What he did amounted to no more than insurance against a possible disaster."[146]

In *Wantulok v. Wantulok*,[147] the Supreme Court of Wyoming adopted a "no harm, no foul" approach to the issue of protection against subsequent creditors. Citing numerous cases, the court said:

"If there were no creditors ..., the conveyance could not be fraudulent as to them. *** Subject thereto, the right of the plaintiff to dispose of his property as he saw proper was absolute and unconditioned. His intent in so doing was wholly immaterial, provided no one but himself was injured or had cause to complain. The statute must have a practical and legal application. It was not the intent [that] the statute should be regarded in the light of a moral code, and operate on the conscience of the party making the conveyance. But its purpose is to protect the legal or equitable rights of others. ... Other authorities, with better reason, we think, hold that, where there is no creditor, there is no fraud, and therefore no policy of the law to prevent the enforcement of the trust. *** The statute does not prohibit conveyances by persons who are not indebted, and no policy of the law is thwarted by a mere motive which cannot work injury to creditors. The motive with which such a conveyance is made and the fears by which it is prompted are of no importance unless there are creditors to be protected by the statute"(Citations omitted).[148]

2. Determination of Intent — "Badges of Fraud"

Under §4(a)(1) of the UFTA, a transfer is a fraudulent transfer if the debtor made the transfer with the *actual intent* to hinder, delay, or defeat the claim of the creditor. **NOTE:** the term "defraud" is usually used as shorthand for "defeat the claim of." Aside from those rare cases where the debtor announces his intent to hinder, delay, or defeat the claim of a creditor, the determination of the debtor's actual intent is made by considering the surrounding facts and circumstances.

Section 4(b) of the UFTA codifies many of these factors, often referred to as "badges of fraud," a term derived from an English case from 1601,[149] and suggests that, in determining actual intent for purposes of §4(a)(1), consideration may be given, among other factors, to whether

(1) the transfer was to an insider;
(2) the debtor retained possession or control of the property transferred after the transfer;
(3) the transfer was disclosed or concealed;
(4) before the transfer was made, the debtor had been sued or threatened with suit;
(5) the transfer was of substantially all the debtor's assets;
(6) the debtor absconded;
(7) the debtor removed or concealed assets;
(8) the value of the consideration received by the debtor was reasonably equivalent to the value of the asset transferred;

(9) the debtor was insolvent or became insolvent shortly after the transfer was made;

(10) the transfer occurred shortly before or shortly after a substantial debt was incurred; and

(11) the debtor transferred the essential assets of the business to a lienor, who transferred the assets to an insider of the debtor.

The foregoing factors include most of the fraudulent transfer intent indicators found by courts over the years in construing and applying the Statute of Elizabeth[150] and section 7 of the Uniform Fraudulent Conveyance Act ("UFCA").[151] The second through the fifth indicators were identified as badges of fraud by Lord Coke in Twyne's Case, as were the use of a trust, and a recitation in the instrument of transfer that it "was made honestly, truly, and bona fide." Thankfully, neither the use of a trust unaccompanied by other badges nor the quoted recitation are now viewed as indicia of fraudulent transfer intent.[152]

Among the above listed badges, the debtor's solvency before and after the transfer is probably the most important. Typically, a transfer will not be held to have been a fraudulent transfer absent proof of actual intent, if, following the transfer, the debtor retained sufficient nonexempt assets to satisfy the claims of his creditors.[153]

Aside from insolvency transfers[154] and undercapitalization transfers,[155] establishing that a transfer was a fraudulent transfer will generally require clear and convincing[156] proof of the debtor's actual intent. Providing asset protection planning services in the context of estate planning or tax planning may go a long way in establishing other, non-creditor hindering motives for the transfer.

3. Effect of a Court Finding a Fraudulent Transfer

If a transfer is found to have been a fraudulent transfer, the creditor has various remedies available, depending upon whether his or her claim is based upon a judgment.[157]

The creditor may seek to have the transfer set aside - undone - as if it never took place. The creditor may also seek an attachment of the transferred asset, (and if the creditor's claim is founded upon a judgment, the court may levy execution on the transferred asset or its proceeds), an injunction against further disposition by the parties, appointment of a receiver to administer the transferred asset (or other property of the transferee), or an order of other appropriate relief.[158]

A court will **not** ordinarily grant injunctive relief to a creditor who does not have a lien on specific property about to be transferred,[159] although such relief has been granted under extreme circumstances.[160]

B. Special Transfer Considerations

1. 18 U.S.C. § 1032: Fraud on the RTC or FDIC

Added by the Crime Control Act of 1990,[161] the broadly written Draconian statute makes it a crime to

> (a)   knowingly conceal or endeavor to conceal an asset or property from the Federal Deposit Insurance Corporation, acting as conservator or receiver or in the Corporation's corporate capacity with respect to any asset acquired or liability assumed by the Corporation under section 11, 12, or 13, of the Federal Deposit Insurance Act (i.e., where the FDIC has taken over a failed bank), the Resolution Trust

Corporation, any conservator appointed by the Comptroller of the Currency or the Director of the Office of Thrift Supervision, or the National Credit Union Administration Board, acting as conservator or liquidating agent;

(b)   corruptly impede or endeavor to impede the functions of such Corporation, Board, or conservators; or

(c)   corruptly place or endeavor to place an asset or property beyond the reach of such Corporation, Board, or conservator.

As part of your due diligence, you should ask your client whether any of his/her obligations are owed to a bank that has been taken over by the FDIC or RTC. If the answer is yes, you must proceed with extreme caution in assisting the client with asset protection planning. If an asset protection trust is to be established, it is recommended that a provision such as the following be included to protect all concerned.

"In addition to the foregoing, it is the Settlor's specific intent not to violate the provisions of §1032 of Title 18 of the US Code. Therefore, with respect to any liability owing, as of the date of execution of this Trust Indenture, to the US Federal Deposit Insurance Corporation (acting as conservator or receiver or in the Corporation's corporate capacity with respect to any asset acquired or liability assumed

Fraudulent Transfers/Conveyances—Voidable Transactions

by the Corporation under §§ 11, 12, or 13 of the Federal Deposit Insurance Act), the Resolution Trust Corporation, or any conservator appointed by the Comptroller of the Currency or the Director of the Office of Thrift Supervision, or the National Credit Union Administration Board (acting as conservator or liquidating agent), where the property (if any) directly securing such debt shall have been liquidated and the proceeds thereof, plus the Settlor's other non-exempt properties (and/or the proceeds thereof), are not, or will not be sufficient to fully satisfy such debt, then, and only in such event, the Trustee hereunder is directed to pay the resulting agreed deficiency directly (and only directly) to such aforementioned Corporation, Board, or conservator from the Trust Estate subject to this Indenture. For purposes of the preceding sentence, the term "agreed deficiency" shall mean that amount agreed to between the Settlor and such Corporation, Board, or conservator as the deficiency which would otherwise exist with respect to such aforementioned debt, absent the preceding sentence. In connection with the foregoing, the Trustee is hereby directed to take whatever action is necessary to accomplish the Settlor's intent as set forth in this paragraph, including, but not limited to, the withdrawal or liquidation of all or a portion of the Trust's capital from any partnership, corporation, or other entity, if, in the opinion of the Trustee, such action is required to comply with the above direction."

It is recommended that a similar provision be adapted for inclusion in a limited partnership or limited liability company agreement.

2. Bankruptcy Issues

It is important for the asset protection planner to have a basic understanding of the federal bankruptcy laws.[162] In particular, the planner should be familiar with the concept of the "property of the bankruptcy estate,"[163] the Bankruptcy Code fraudulent conveyance rules,[164] the rule which permits the debtor (in some states) to choose between utilizing his or her state's exemptions or the federal exemptions,[165] the meaning of "insolvency" under the Bankruptcy Code,[166] and, importantly, the circumstances under which a bankruptcy discharge will be denied.[167]

In the unfortunate circumstance where one must go through bankruptcy, the goal of the ordeal is to obtain a fresh start - a discharge in bankruptcy.[168] One should not implement asset protection planning if bankruptcy is contemplated (the planner should obtain a written representation from the client to that effect). However, even if your client has no thought of bankruptcy when implementing asset protection planning, circumstances can change. Therefore, the planner must be cognizant of what actions a client might take that could result in a denial of the bankruptcy discharge.

Section 727(a) of the Bankruptcy Code provides, in relevant part: "(a) the court shall grant the debtor a discharge, unless -

***

(2) the debtor, with intent to hinder, delay, or defraud a creditor or an officer of the estate charged with custody of property under this

title, has transferred, removed, destroyed, mutilated, or concealed, or has permitted to be transferred, removed, destroyed, mutilated, or concealed --

(A) property of the debtor, within one year before the date of the filing of the petition; ..."

The courts are generally split on the nature of the debtor's conduct required to manifest the intent required by §727(a)(2) to deny a discharge. However, a tactic that often gets debtors into trouble in the area of pre-bankruptcy planning is "eleventh hour" conversions of nonexempt assets into exempt assets,[169] even though such conversions were favorably contemplated by Congress in enacting the Bankruptcy Code. The committee reports (House and Senate) accompanying §522 both provide:

> "As under current law, the debtor will be permitted to convert nonexempt property into exempt property before filing a bankruptcy petition. The practice is not fraudulent as to creditors, and permits the debtor to make full use of the exemptions to which he is entitled under the law."[170]

Notwithstanding what appears to be explicit language in the Congressional committee reports allowing the pre-bankruptcy conversion of non-exempt assets into exempt assets, the courts continue to deny discharges where fraudulent transfer intent is found in connection with the conversion.[171] The cases are somewhat difficult to reconcile, and the planner must therefore carefully analyze each matter on the basis of the facts and circumstances before him (or her).

Finally, §152 of the Bankruptcy Code makes it a felony to fraudulently transfer or conceal property with the intent to defeat the provisions of the Bankruptcy Code.

3. <u>Other Special Considerations</u>

The Money Laundering Control Act[172] (the "Act") was enacted in 1986 as part of the Anti-Drug Abuse Act of 1986[173] to provide an additional means of prosecuting drug traffickers. Section 1956(a)(1) of the Act provides:

"(a)(1) Whoever, knowing that the property involved in a financial transaction represents the proceeds of some form of unlawful activity, conducts or attempts to conduct such a financial transaction which in fact involves the proceeds of specified unlawful activity --

(A) (i) with the intent to promote the carrying on of specified unlawful activity; or

(ii) with intent to engage in conduct constituting a violation of section 7201 or 7206 of the Internal Revenue Code of 1986; or

(B) knowing that the transaction is designed in whole or in part ---

(i) to conceal or disguise the nature, the location, the source, the ownership, or the control of the proceeds of specified unlawful activity; or

(ii) to avoid a transaction reporting requirement under State or Federal law, shall be sentenced to a fine of not more than $500,000 or twice the value of the property involved in the transaction, whichever is greater, or imprisonment for not more than twenty years, or both."

Subsection (a)(2) and (a)(3) make it unlawful to move funds into or out of the United States, or to conduct or attempt to conduct a financial transaction with the intent to promote the carrying on of a

Fraudulent Transfers/Conveyances—Voidable Transactions

"specified unlawful activity,"[174] or to move such funds, or to conduct or attempt to conduct a financial transaction, having been informed by a law enforcement officer that such funds represent the proceeds of some form of unlawful activity, and knowing that such movement was designed to conceal or disguise the nature, location, source, ownership, or the control of the proceeds of a specified unlawful activity, or to avoid state or federal reporting requirements.

In addition to the severe criminal sanctions provided in §1956(a),[175] §1956(b) authorizes the imposition of civil penalties,[176] the burden of proof for which is the lower "preponderance of the evidence" standard, rather than the criminal standard requiring proof "beyond a reasonable doubt."

Section 1957 also makes it unlawful to knowingly engage in a "monetary transaction" involving proceeds in excess of $10,000 derived from a specified unlawful activity.

Asset protection planning, and, to a large extent, everyday estate planning, typically involve transfers of property, gifts, and other financial transactions. Thus, the planner must exercise due diligence to assure himself or herself that the planning to be undertaken for the client will not result in a violation of §§ 1956 or 1957, particularly since the Congressional history of the Act indicates that the knowledge requirement could be met by a showing of "willful blindness,"[177] which could be inferred from evidence of out-of-the-ordinary dealings or transactions.

CHAPTER VI

EXEMPTION PLANNING—STATE LAW PROVIDED ASSET PROTECTION

In this context, a property interest that is referred to as "exempt" is generally not reachable by a creditor. This section highlights property exemptions that are available under federal law and under the laws of some states and offers planning suggestions in connection with securing and maximizing the effectiveness of such exemptions. *Each exemption statute must be carefully examined to determine from which creditors the property is exempt and the amount of the property that is exempt.*

A. Homestead Exemption

Homestead exemptions in the United States vary as widely as the states themselves, ranging from no exemption,[178] minimum value exemptions,[179] to unlimited value exemptions, restricted by the size of the property involved.[180]

If a state provides a homestead exemption, the law will exempt a portion or all of the value of a principal residence from claims of most creditors of the owner and sometimes also the heirs of the owner.[181]

Qualification for the exemption similarly varies from state to state, ranging from being a "natural person,"[182] to being a "head of a family,"[183] and so on.

In those states where the homestead exemption is unavailable, or where it is severely limited in amount, one may consider the use of a "split purchase" technique for the property. Under a basic structure utilizing this strategy, a life estate[184] in real property to be used as a personal residence is acquired by the life tenant simultaneously with a remainder interest being acquired by other persons, each party providing fair and adequate consideration.[185] Some protection will be afforded through the utilization of this technique as a result of the limited interests held by each of the parties. That is, of what value is a life estate in a personal residence to a creditor?

The split purchase transaction may be subject to US generation skipping tax (although currently the tax law provides a very large GST exemption, making this unlikely),[186] depending upon the parties involved, and could possibly result in adverse gift tax consequences unless it is structured to constitute a personal residence trust.[187] In any event, the use of a trust is recommended to overcome a loss of creditor protection, vis-à-vis the remainderman, upon the death of the term holder.

If a state does provide a strong homestead exemption, and if it would not constitute a fraudulent transfer[188] and would otherwise make sense, the planner may advise the client to pay down or pay off mortgages encumbering the homestead property. This technique will have the effect of converting non-exempt assets into exempt property, albeit non-income producing exempt property.

B. Wage Account Exemptions

Although the Federal Consumer Credit Protection Act[189] does provide a limitation[190] on the amount of the disposable earnings of an individual that may be garnished, the federal statute has been construed not to include the exemption of such earnings when deposited into a bank or financial institution account.[191] The statute has been further construed to only apply to wage garnishments affecting an employer-employee relationship.[192] The federal wage exemption, and many of the state wage exemptions, are overridden by support orders and obligations, bankruptcy court orders, and state and federal tax debts.[193] Florida has expanded the exemption otherwise afforded by the federal statute by providing that the disposable earnings of the head of a family are 100 percent exempt, regardless of the amount, and *remain exempt* for six months after being deposited into an account at a financial institution.[194] In addition, Florida's law provides an account exemption for a non-head of a family in line with the limitations of the federal act.[195]

Since the federal statute has been interpreted to only include wages resulting from an employer-employee relationship, and considering the lack of agreement among state courts on the issue,[196] where it would not constitute a fraudulent transfer or violate other laws, the planner may recommend that if the client is an independent contractor, he or she incorporate and adopt an appropriate employment agreement in order to create an employer-employee relationship, and thereby constitute the income payments to the client from the corporation as potentially creditor-exempt wages.

C. Annuity Exemptions

Several states[197] provide that the proceeds of annuity contracts are exempt from the claims of creditors. These exemptions vary significantly between the states, but none of the exemptions appear as broad as Florida's. In *In Re Mart*,[198] the bankruptcy court held that Florida's annuity exemption[199] applied to an annuity purchased by the debtors (thirteen months before filing their bankruptcy petition) from an irrevocable trust nominally settled by their daughter the day before the annuity transaction.

In *McCollam v. McCollam*,[200] an insurance company, *in lieu of a lump sum payment*, established an annuity for Mrs. McCollam as part of a settlement for her father's wrongful death. Four years later, Mrs. McCollam filed a petition in bankruptcy, wherein she claimed an exemption for the settlement annuity.

Upon receipt of an opinion of law requested from the Supreme Court of Florida,[201] the federal Eleventh Circuit court affirmed the lower court's order holding the settlement contract exempt as an annuity.[202]

D. Qualified Retirement Plans/IRA's

1. Qualified Plans

Whether a debtor's interest in an ERISA qualified retirement plan[203] was exempt from bankruptcy distribution had been the subject of much uncertainty across the United States until the Supreme Court decision in *Patterson v. Shumate*.[204] The issue had centered around Bankruptcy Code § 541, which defines the items of the debtor's property that are included in the bankruptcy estate (and thus used to pay the bankrupt person's creditors), and which excludes from the bankruptcy estate the interest of the debtor in a trust subject to a spendthrift provision enforceable under "applicable nonbankruptcy law." The confusion had been the construction of the quoted phrase - some courts had held that it only referred to state law and that since ERISA (a federal law) overrode such state law, there was no spendthrift protection; other courts had held that the

ERISA required anti-alienation (spendthrift) provision qualified as applicable nonbankruptcy law, and there was effective spendthrift protection.[205]

Joseph Shumate Jr. had been employed for over thirty years by the Coleman Furniture Corporation. He participated, along with four hundred others, in the company's pension plan. The plan satisfied the applicable ERISA requirements and qualified for favorable tax treatment under the Internal Revenue Code. Among other ERISA-required provisions contained in the plan, it contained an anti-alienation (spendthrift) provision that provided that benefits under the plan could not be assigned or alienated (transferred). Shumate's interest in the plan was valued at $250,000.

The company and Shumate separately filed for protection under the Bankruptcy Code. As part of the company's proceeding, its bankruptcy trustee terminated and liquidated its pension plan, providing full distribution to all participants except Shumate. Shumate's bankruptcy trustee (Patterson) sued to compel the distribution of Shumate's plan interest to him for use in paying Shumate's creditors. Shumate argued that the ERISA-required anti-alienation provision contained in the plan was a restriction on transfer enforceable under applicable non-bankruptcy law, and, as such, should result in the exclusion of his plan interest from the bankruptcy estate. Patterson argued that the Bankruptcy Code reference to "non-bankruptcy law" should be interpreted to mean only such provisions as were enforceable under state law, and *not* federal law such as ERISA.

In a *unanimous decision*, the US Supreme Court held that "applicable non-bankruptcy law" is not limited to state law, stating: "Plainly read, the provision encompasses any relevant non-bankruptcy law, including federal law such as ERISA."[206] Referring to Bankruptcy

Code Section 541, the Court said that "The test contains no limitation on 'applicable non-bankruptcy law' relating to the source of the law..."[207]

In support of its holding, the Court stated that its decision will ensure that the protection of pension benefits will not vary based upon the beneficiary's bankruptcy status; give full and appropriate effect to ERISA's goal of protecting pension benefits; and ensure that the security of a debtor's pension benefits will be governed by ERISA, and not left to the vagaries of state spendthrift laws.

Several lower court cases have subsequently eroded *Patterson's* seemingly all-encompassing holding.

In *In Re Witwer*,[208] the debtor was the sole shareholder and only employee of his corporation. Upon filing for bankruptcy relief under Chapter 7, he wanted to keep his $1.8 million profit-sharing plan interest out of the hands of the bankruptcy trustee.

The court, citing a Labor Department regulation,[209] held that a sole owner of a corporation was not an employee (even though employment taxes were paid as they would have been for any employee) and could not therefore be an ERISA qualified plan participant (since only an "employee" can be a plan participant), and the court distinguished *Patterson* on that basis.

In *In Re Lane*,[210] the debtor, a self-employed dentist, filed a petition for relief under Chapter 7 of the Bankruptcy Code. The dentist maintained two Keogh plans, and even though he did employ unrelated persons in his practice, he made no contributions to the plans on behalf of any of them.

The court held that neither Keogh plan was an ERISA qualified plan, both having failed to meet the non-discrimination tests prescribed by the Internal Revenue Code.[211] The court went on to hold that non-qualified plans are not eligible for exemption under New York law, which recognizes spendthrift provisions in such plans as if the trust were a spendthrift trust established by another person for the beneficiary. Since New York law does not recognize self-settled spendthrift trusts, Dr. Lane's "Keogh" plan interests were not exempt.

Based upon the foregoing, the following rules can be derived: A non-owner participant's interest in an ERISA qualified plan will be excluded from his/her bankruptcy estate and will not otherwise be reachable by creditors; a sole owner-participant's interest in an ERISA qualified plan may be an asset of the bankruptcy estate; depending upon the laws of the debtor's state,[212] may or may not be reachable by creditors outside of bankruptcy; and a non-sole owner-participant's interest (where persons other than the owner-participant's spouse are the other shareholders) in an ERISA qualified plan that includes non-owner participants will be excluded from the bankruptcy estate and exempt under state law as well.

It seems that in a short time we have come "full circle": from a muddled area of the law - to seeming clarification - to (again) a muddled area of the law.

2. Individual Retirement Accounts

Individual Retirement Accounts ("IRA's") are not ERISA plans and therefore are not covered by the *Patterson* case. Various state laws do, however, exempt IRAs from creditor claims.[213] *See* section IV D 6, above, for a discussion of enhanced protection of IRA assets.

3. Federal Tax Claims

Although not entirely clear, it is likely that a federal tax lien will take precedence over the ERISA exemptions, particularly where the federal tax lien is filed prior to a bankruptcy petition.[214]

E. Other Exemptions

1. Life Insurance

Many states provide exemptions for the cash surrender value and/or for the death benefit proceeds of life insurance contracts.[215]

Some states limit the "proceeds" exemptions to proceeds payable to the insured's spouse or dependent,[216] and several states exempt policy cash surrender values.[217]

Each state's statutes must be examined to determine (1) the extent of the exemption - are policy proceeds and/or cash values exempt from the insured's creditors, the beneficiary's creditors, or both; (2) exceptions to the exemption, and whether the exemption is in addition to, or included in, the other personal property exemptions provided by state law.

In those states that do not provide an effective or satisfactory exemption for life insurance, a viable alternative[218] is an irrevocable life insurance trust. Since the typical life insurance trust structure will involve an absolute transfer by the insured of the policy and its attendant rights, with no controls ("incidents of ownership") retained by the insured, the technique may provide effective asset protection for the cash surrender value of the policy during the insured's lifetime, and for the proceeds of the matured policy following the insured's death, to the extent such funds remain subject to appropriate spendthrift, discretionary distribution, or other protective trust provisions. An offshore trust is not necessary, except perhaps where the policy transferor is not the insured and desires to retain benefits from the policy.[219]

2. Miscellaneous Exemptions

The state exemption statutes provide that various items of personal property are exempt from creditors' claims. These items range from a family bible to one shotgun or musket.

CHAPTER VII

OFFSHORE TRUST ENVIRONMENT — OVERVIEW OF SELECTED JURISDICTIONS

A. Common-Law Jurisdictions

1. Cook Islands

a. General information.

The Cook Islands is an English speaking, independent, sovereign member of the British Commonwealth, in free association with New Zealand.[220] Rarotonga, the most populated island, is located in the South Pacific approximately nineteen hundred miles northeast of Auckland, New Zealand, and approximately forty-seven hundred miles southwest of Los Angeles. The fifteen islands comprising this country are far from the world's financial centers, but do have modern communication facilities in operation twenty-four hours a day, including a cellular telephone network. The legal system of the Cook Islands is an English common-law system. International trusts are exempt from tax in the Cook Islands.

b. Legislation and other items of note.

As alluded to throughout this book, the Cook Islands has enacted what may fairly be described as the most comprehensive asset protection trust legislation in the world.[221] The highlights of the legislation include an effective zero statute of limitations on fraudulent transfers where the transferor is solvent after the transfer, a maximum two-year statute of limitations in other cases, requiring proof of a fraudulent transfer "beyond a reasonable doubt,"[222] provisions permitting the establishment of self-settled spendthrift trusts,[223] provisions validating trusts where the settlor has retained significant powers,[224] choice of governing law provisions,[225] a non-recognition of foreign judgments provision,[226] and even a section that provides that community property transferred to an international trust retains its character as community property.[227]

Also of note is the fact that the Cook Islands does not have bankruptcy legislation, and that the International Trusts Act 1984 does in fact provide that the settlor's bankruptcy will not render the international trust void or voidable.[228]

2. Cayman Islands

a. General information.

The Cayman Islands are a British Crown Colony located in the western Caribbean, approximately five hundred miles south of Miami, Florida. The Cayman Islands are easily accessible from Miami, English is the official language, and, of course, its legal system is based on the English common law.

The Cayman Islands currently impose no income tax, capital gain tax, wealth tax, withholding tax, gift tax, or inheritance tax, and an exempt trust can obtain a fifty-year guarantee that such exemption will continue.

b. Legislation and other items of note.

The trust laws of the Cayman Islands are considered to be comprised of the Trusts Law, the Fraudulent Dispositions Law, the Perpetuities Law, the Property (Miscellaneous Provisions) Law 1994, and the Special Trusts (Alternative Regime) Law 1997. The Cayman Islands are not a party to the Hague Convention[229] and have no present plans to become a party.

The laws of the Cayman Islands provide a <u>six-year statute of limitations on fraudulent transfers</u> (two years longer than the Uniform Fraudulent Transfer Act),[230] and a fraudulent transfer is only set aside to the extent necessary to satisfy the claim of the creditor bringing the action.[231]

The Cayman Islands do have bankruptcy laws that provide, *among other things*, that a trust is voidable by the trustee in bankruptcy when the bankruptcy order is made within two years of the settlement, or when the bankruptcy order is made within **ten years** of the settlement of the trust, unless (placing the burden on the settlor) it can be proved that, at the time of settlement, the settlor was able to pay his debts without having to utilize the assets transferred to the trust, and that the settlor's interest in the trust property had been effectively conveyed to the trustee upon execution of the settlement.[232]

Although the Cayman Islands have strict secrecy laws,[233] it has entered into the Mutual Legal Assistance Treaty with the United States. Under this agreement, Cayman will supply information to the United States in connection with certain drug investigations and white-collar crimes. In addition, the Cayman Islands also have a tax information exchange agreement with the United States.

3. Gibraltar

   a. General information.

Gibraltar is a tiny British Territory connected to the southern tip of the Iberian peninsula, approximately twenty miles off the northern tip of Africa.

It is readily accessible via air service from London and has modern communication facilities, including a computer system by which one can check to determine if a proposed company name is already in use. Gibraltar is an English common-law jurisdiction, and although English is the official language, many inhabitants also speak Spanish.

Trusts established by non-residents that exclude residents of Gibraltar as beneficiaries are exempt from Gibraltar income tax.

   b. Legislation and other items of note.

Trust legislation in Gibraltar is generally based on the trust law of the United Kingdom. Thus, Gibraltar recognizes and gives full effect to the concept of the trust. The Trustee Act of Gibraltar is the main governing Act. It is based on the Trustee Act 1893 of the United Kingdom, as amended. In 1989, Gibraltar introduced the Trusts (Recognition) Act. This applies to Gibraltar the provisions of the Convention on the Law Applicable to Trusts and their Recognition agreed at The Hague in October 1984.

The Bankruptcy Ordinance (as amended in 1990), Gibraltar's principal asset protection statute, provides that a creditor cannot reach trust assets on fraudulent transfer grounds if, at the date of settlement of the trust, the settlor was solvent and did not become insolvent by virtue of the settlement.[234] Thus, if these tests are met, there should be no fraudulent transfer concern under Gibraltar law in establishing a Gibraltar registered trust.

4. Isle of Man

a. General information.

The Isle of Man[235] is a self-governing territory located in the Irish Sea, equidistant from England, Scotland, and Ireland. The Isle was discovered in 800 CE, and, except for about a century, has been a possession of British nobility since 1405. The Isle has an advanced communications system, including a cellular telephone network. It is easily accessible by air from London, Manchester, Liverpool, Blackpool, Dublin, and Belfast. It has an English common-law legal system, and English is the spoken and written language.

The Isle's bicameral legislative body is more than a thousand years old, providing a significant degree of political stability, and the country is also financially stable.

b. Legislation and other items of note.

The trust law in the Isle of Man is based on, but is not identical to, the trust law of England. The Isle's trust laws are comprised of the Trustee Act 1961, the Variation of Trusts Act 1961, the Perpetuities and Accumulations Act 1968, and the Recognition of Trusts Act 1988, which incorporates the Hague Convention as part of the Isle's trust laws, the Trusts Act 1995, the Purpose Trusts Act 1996, and the Trustee Act 2001.

Manx trust law provides that a trust "shall be governed by the law chosen by the settlor." Planners have utilized this provision to establish trusts in the Isle of Man that are governed by the laws of a jurisdiction with more favorable trust protection laws, such as the Cook Islands. This technique permits the planner to realize the benefit of combining the political, economic, and legal stability of the Isle of Man (probably the most stable trust jurisdiction in the world) with comprehensive and protective trust legislation from elsewhere in the world.

5. The Bahamas

a. General information.

The Bahamas is an archipelago of almost seven hundred islands extending from sixty miles east of Palm Beach, Florida, to just north of Haiti. English is the official language of this common-law member of the British Commonwealth. The Bahamas was settled around 1640 by a group of Englishmen from Bermuda, and it has had a representative form of government since the seventeenth century. It has existed as an independent country, within the Commonwealth, since 1973. The Bahamas does not impose an income tax on offshore trusts.

b. Legislation and other items of note.

In an effort to promote itself as an asset protection trust jurisdiction, The Bahamas fraudulent transfer law provides a two-year statute of limitations on bringing a fraudulent transfer claim and places the burden of establishing the settlor's fraudulent transfer intent on the creditor seeking to set aside the transfer. Other Bahamian trust-related legislation includes the Trustee Act 1893, the Trustee Act

1998, the Trusts (Choice of Governing Law) Act 1989, and the Trusts (Choice of Governing Law) (Amendment) Act 1996. It is interesting to note that although Bahamian trust law permits a settlor to be a beneficiary of a Bahamian trust, a settlor will not be protected by a spendthrift provision in his/her trust. This seems incongruous if the country is seeking asset protection trust business.

6. Belize

a. General information.

Belize (formerly British Honduras) is the only Central American member of the British Commonwealth. English is its official language, and its legal system is English common law-based. Belize became an independent republic in 1981 and has been internally politically stable since then; however, it does have an ongoing border dispute with Guatemala.

A trust established by a non-resident settlor for non-resident beneficiaries is not subject to Belizian income, estate, or gift taxes.[236]

b. Legislation and other items of note.

The Trusts Act 1992 contains a 120-year rule against perpetuities,[237] specific validation of self-settled spendthrift trusts,[238] an explicit trust protector provision,[239] and a comprehensive governing law provision that not only permits the settlor to choose the governing law of the trust but also permits the terms of the trust to be severed and each severed section to be subject to different governing laws.[240]

Section 7 of the Act provides - *without a two year or any other waiting period* - that the Belizian Court shall not set aside a trust created under its laws, recognize any claim against the assets of the trust, or the order of a court of another jurisdiction respecting the trust, *with regard to* marriage, divorce, forced heirship, *and creditor claims in the event of the settlor's insolvency.*[241] The foregoing provision applies notwithstanding the general Belizian fraudulent transfer laws, its bankruptcy laws, and its international reciprocity laws.[242] The foregoing provision is touted as being a "zero" statute of limitations on claims seeking to reach the assets of a Belize trust; ***however***, although the restrictions upon the Court are generous, the types of claims that can't be pursued are actually limited. Only marital claims, estate claims, and claims from creditors in an insolvency are barred. *All other types of creditor claims for fraudulent transfer may be brought against a Belize international trust.*

7. Turks and Caicos Islands

a. General information.

The Turks and Caicos Islands are a British Colony located in the West Indies approximately 575 miles from Miami, Florida. The Islands are easily accessible via daily air service from Miami, and air service is also available from Nassau, Haiti, and the Dominican Republic. Communication services are modern. English is the official language, and it has an English common law-based legal system. The Islands do not impose an income tax and do not, therefore, have in effect any tax treaties.

b. Legislation and other items of note.

The English common-law concept of the trust has existed in the Islands since 1799. English trust law developments since that time are applied in the Islands except where modified by local legislation.

Trust legislation in the Islands is principally contained in the Trust Ordinance 1990.

Key provisions of the Ordinance are a comprehensive governing law provision, which, like that of Belize, permits the settlor to choose the governing law and permits specification that the laws of different jurisdictions will apply to severable portions of the trust;[243] a provision permitting trusts of perpetual duration;[244] and an asset protection "lock" provision, similar to Gibraltar's, precluding creditor attack against a trust on fraudulent transfer grounds if the settlor is a solvent individual when the transfer is made to the trust and is not thereby rendered insolvent.[245]

8. Nevis

a. General information.

Nevis is the smaller of two islands comprising the Federation of St. Christopher ("St. Kitts") and Nevis (collectively, the "Federation"). Nevis is located in the Eastern Caribbean, approximately thirteen hundred miles southwest of Miami, Florida. The capital is Charlestown. Nevis, an English-speaking common-law jurisdiction with modern communications facilities and established professional trust services, has about nine thousand residents. The Federation became an independent member of the British Commonwealth in 1983, under a constitution granting Nevis autonomy and the right to its own legislative and executive functions. In 1993, the Federation's opposition to offshore legislation strained relations between St. Kitts and Nevis. An interesting fact about Nevis is that Alexander Hamilton, the first Secretary of the Treasury of the United States, was born in Charlestown, Nevis.

b. Legislation and other items of note.

The Nevis International Exempt Trust Ordinance of 1994 ("Ordinance"), effective April 28, 1994 (amended in 2000), constitutes the Nevis asset protection trust law. The Ordinance was modeled after the Cook Islands International Trusts Act 1984 (the "Cook Islands Act"). The Ordinance permits self-settled spendthrift trusts, prohibits forced heirship, and abolishes the common-law rule against perpetuities. The Ordinance exempts international trust assets and income from income, corporation, gift, withholding, estate, asset inheritance, succession, and stamp taxes in Nevis.

An interesting aspect of the Nevis law is that a creditor seeking relief against a Nevis asset protection trust will be required to post a $25,000 bond with the Nevis court in order to proceed with a lawsuit.

9. Liechtenstein

a. General information.

Liechtenstein is a tiny civil-law principality located between Switzerland and Austria on the upper Rhine River. The country was established in 1719, has enjoyed political and economic stability since the end of World War II, and boasts the third highest per capita income in the world. Liechtenstein has an excellent communications system and is easily accessible by car or train from Zurich.

Although the official language is German, English is spoken by many inhabitants and is used in commercial transactions and communications. Liechtenstein is a civil law jurisdiction. It, like Switzerland, has strict bank secrecy laws, although since the enactment of FATCA,[246] that fact seems illusory.

b. <u>Legislation and other items of note.</u>

Since Liechtenstein is a civil-law jurisdiction, the common-law concept of the trust does not exist. Therefore, legislation was required to create the trust concept in Liechtenstein law. That legislation was enacted in 1926 and is codified in Articles 897–932 of the Personen- Und Gesellschaftsrecht of 20 January 1926, ("PGR"). Since the trust concept is not part of the civil law, the PGR addresses a wide array of trust issues.

Regarding fraudulent transfers, if at the time of transferring assets to the trust the settlor was solvent and had no creditors with unsatisfied claims, the trust cannot be attacked.[247] If there are creditors, and the settlor becomes insolvent within one year of a transfer to a trust, and the creditor's claim remains unsatisfied, or if the trust was established with the intent to defraud creditors (and this intent was known to the trustee and the beneficiary), then such creditors may challenge the trust within a five-year period. Liechtenstein does not grant comity to foreign judgments. Therefore, a creditor with a foreign judgment must bring the action *de novo* in Liechtenstein, and in order to do so, must deposit into the court 10–15 percent of the amount of the judgment sought to be satisfied.

Liechtenstein trusts are not subject to a rule against perpetuities or accumulations. Section 931 of the PGR permits the creation of a Liechtenstein trust governed by the law of another jurisdiction.

Such a provision can be useful where a European trust situs is necessary, while permitting the use of trust laws that are more protective than local law. PGR Section 931 requires the foreign governing law to be set forth in detail in the trust.

CHAPTER VIII

SOURCES OF LIABILITY

At the beginning of this book, a tongue-in-cheek reference was made to the possibility of a supermarket chain being sued for selling red meat to someone who then developed coronary artery disease. While no case on that point has been found, the sources from which liability may arise are numerous and varied, and they seem to be expanding exponentially.

This section will highlight the major sources of liability that may result in an impairment of the financial condition of an individual or an entity. The focus will be from the source - categorized by type of creditor.

A. Tort Creditors

This category of source is probably the most encompassing, although with the pace at which Congress passes laws creating regulatory agencies (which agencies in turn promulgate regulation upon regulation), regulatory liability is assuredly "in the running" for most encompassing sources.

Professionals - physicians, attorneys, accountants, architects, engineers, and the like, tend to narrowly view this source in terms of their malpractice exposure. This area is often thought of as the prime focus of asset protection planning. Although protection from the future potential tort creditor is often sought, properly structured and implemented, asset protection planning offers far broader protection than only from tort creditors. Certainly, the professional may wish to address that issue, but he or she should also be aware of tort creditor exposure from other obvious sources, including those risks believed to be insured, particularly in view of the possibility of liability insurer failure (i.e., the insurance company won't be there when you need them), or a denial (or avoidance) of coverage. In addition, one should be cognizant of those circumstances that may negate the effectiveness of traditional entity protection features, and, for example, permit tort liability to "pierce the corporate veil."

A story that aired on the July 6, 1993, NBC show *Dateline* illustrates just how out of hand tort liability can get. A retired couple, Mr. and Mrs. Howard, were on a motor vacation in Idaho. They were towing a car behind their RV, and because of the relatively large size of the RV, they could not see the towed car in their rearview mirror. A tire on the car blew out, but since the Howards could not see it, they drove on. The tire disintegrated, leaving the car riding on a metal rim. The metal rim's contact with the pavement caused sparks to fly, setting fire to roadside trees, resulting in the destruction of sixty-two hundred acres of timberland -- all unbeknownst to Mr. and Mrs. Howard. On that *Dateline* show, the State of Idaho indicated that it intended to sue the Howards for more than $1 million in damages and that it would not hesitate to go after all of their assets, including their available retirement savings. The Howards' net worth was well below the amount of damages sought by Idaho. The Howard case illustrates how tort liability can be imposed on individuals from truly unimagined claimants.[248]

A relatively new tort creditor source (also a regulatory creditor source) arises from fracking. Fracking (hydraulic fracturing) is a drilling process that was first commercially used in 1949, and one whose use has exploded in recent years. Fracking involves forcing fluid at high pressure into a geologic formation containing oil or gas. The fluid fractures the formation, allowing oil and gas to flow to the wellbore (the hole drilled for extraction). Our decades of providing asset protection representation enables us to clearly see the handwriting on the wall: *the litigation storm from fracking is coming.* These claims are likely to take the form of public nuisance claims arising from seismic activity caused by fracturing, wrongful death claims arising from gas accumulation explosions in residences and businesses, strict liability, negligence, and recklessness claims arising from medical conditions caused by fracking chemical runoff and natural gas leaks, subsurface trespass claims, landowner-lessors' liability for damage caused to neighboring properties and residents. Current fracking-related litigation has focused on the oil companies operating the wells as defendants. It won't be too long before plaintiffs realize that it would be easier, cheaper, and more expeditious to sue the landowner (who leased his property to the oil company). After all, the landowner is unlikely to possess the litigation-delaying resources of the oil companies.

B. Regulatory Creditors

1. Environmental Creditors

Our environmental protection statutes are a significant source of regulatory liability for individuals and entities, approaching (if not representing) strict liability[249] in their Draconian application.

Sources Of Liability

The primary environmental liability statute is CERCLA, the Comprehensive Environmental Response, Compensation, and Liability Act of 1980, often referred to as "Superfund."[250]

The liabilities with which one may be faced from environmental sources tend to be enormous and tend to defy traditional notions of entity liability insulation. For example, under Superfund, officers, directors, and even shareholders[251] of corporations may be liable for corporate environmental wrongdoing, as might a trustee be held personally liable with respect to the environmental problems of property owned by the trust he, she, or it is administering.[252] Such liability may be imposed even where a prior owner released the toxic substances resulting in the problem.

2. Other Regulatory Creditors

Of note in this area is the Office of Thrift Supervision/Kaye, Scholer matter.[253] Although one of the issues in this matter was malpractice, the other issues were regulatory related. Noteworthy about the matter was an OTS freeze order, barring the law firm and its partners from disposing of assets without receiving adequate consideration.

The Federal Trade Commission and the SEC also issue "freeze" orders.

The Employee Retirement Income Security Act of 1974 ("ERISA") imposes personal liability on retirement plan fiduciaries who breach their fiduciary duties.[254] In addition to the plan trustees, who are obviously fiduciaries in the common-law sense, any person who exercises discretion in the management of assets, renders investment advice for a fee, or possesses discretionary authority with regard to the administration of a retirement plan is a fiduciary for ERISA purposes.[255] Thus, one who satisfies the ERISA definition of a fiduciary may be held personally liable under that Act.

Asset protection planning, undertaken at a time when transfers would not constitute fraudulent transfers, can be effective in such regulatory cases.

C. Contract Creditors

The term being almost self-explanatory, individuals and entities may be exposed to liability arising from the breach of, or an obligation incurred under a contract, including the calling upon personal guarantees of a shareholder or partner. Because of the potential for exposure to environmental liability, mortgage lenders prefer to take initial action against a guarantor when a loan is defaulted, rather than foreclose on the underlying real property or accept the property via a deed in lieu of foreclosure. In some such instances, properly undertaken asset protection planning can redirect the lender's focus toward the primary real estate collateral.[256]

D. Marital Creditors

An individual's assets will generally be exposed to the claims of his or her spouse in a divorce action to one degree or another. Even carefully drafted premarital agreements can be set aside, indicating that *unilateral premarital asset protection planning would be advisable* where any concern over potential marital exposure exists. In some states, even postmarital asset protection planning may be undertaken, but it must be remembered that any asset protection planning becomes more venerable with age.

CHAPTER IX

US REPORTING REQUIREMENTS

A. Gift Tax

Typically, the transfer of assets to an asset protection trust will be structured as an "incomplete gift" for federal gift tax purposes (that means the transfer of assets to the asset protection trust will not constitute a "gift" for US federal gift tax purposes, even though in the everyday world of real-life, it will). This is accomplished by the settlor (creator of the trust) retaining a limited power of appointment over the trust - a power to direct the trustee to transfer assets to certain beneficiaries. Although no gift tax is due on an incomplete gift, the Regulations do require informational reporting.[257]

> "If the donor contends that a power is of such nature as to render the gift incomplete, and hence not subject to the tax as of the "calendar period" ... of the initial transfer, the transaction shall be disclosed in the return and evidence showing all relevant facts, including a copy of the instrument of transfer, should be submitted."[258]

B. Income Tax

1. Limited Partnership

Although no income tax is paid by the partnership, a US limited partnership is required to file an annual *informational* federal income tax return on Form 1065.[259] A limited liability company with more than one member (owner) may be treated as a partnership. If so, it will also be required to file Form 1065.

2. Asset Protection Trust

As discussed elsewhere in these materials, the typical asset protection trust will be a grantor trust[260] for US income tax purposes. As such, the Regulations require the income, deductions, and credits of the trust to be reported on a separate statement attached to the trust's *informational* income tax return, which will be either Form 1041 or 1040NR (also discussed below).[261] No US income tax is payable by a grantor trust itself; however, the trust's items of income, deduction, and credit shown on the statement attached to its Form 1041 or 1040NR are required to be reported on the settlor's income tax return.[262]

C. Other

The term "owner" is used in US tax law in reference to certain trusts. Under the common law of trusts (and under property law), there is no such thing as an owner of the trust. However, US income tax law creates a legal fiction that a person (usually the settlor) is an "owner" of a certain type of trust, referred to as a "grantor trust." These rules are referred to as the grantor trust rules,[263] mentioned above. *The fact that the tax law designates a person as an owner of a trust has no effect on the asset protection otherwise afforded by the trust, and that tax law designation does not make a person the "owner" of a trust for any other purpose whatsoever.*

1. Foreign Trust Information Reporting

   a. Form 3520.

If the asset protection trust is a "foreign trust" for US income tax purposes, IRS Form 3520 must be filed by the settlor on or before the date the income tax return of the settlor is due (including extensions). Thus, for an individual settlor, Form 3520 is due by April 15, and for most entity settlors, by the seventy-fifth day after the close of the tax year of the entity settlor (March 15 for a calendar year entity settlor).[264] This filing is required regardless of whether the trust is a grantor trust.[265] A penalty generally applies if Form 3520 is not timely filed or if the information is incomplete or incorrect. Generally, the initial penalty is equal to the **greater of** $10,000 or 35 percent of the gross value of any property transferred to a foreign trust for failure by a US transferor to report the creation of or transfer to a foreign trust or 35 percent of the gross value of the distributions received from a foreign trust for failure by a US person to report receipt of the distribution or 5 percent of the gross value of the portion of the trust's assets treated as owned by a US person for failure by the US person to report the US owner information.

Additional penalties will be imposed if the noncompliance continues after the IRS mails a notice of failure to comply with the required reporting.

b. Form 3520-A.

Form 3520-A is the annual information return of a foreign trust with at least one US tax "owner". The form provides information about the foreign trust, its US beneficiaries, and any US person who is treated as an owner of any portion of the foreign trust for US income tax purposes. Unlike the 3520, which is filed by the settlor of the trust, the foreign trust itself must file Form 3520-A in order for the US owner to satisfy its annual information reporting requirements under the Internal Revenue Code.[266] Each US person treated as an owner of any portion of a foreign trust under the grantor trust rules is responsible for ensuring that the foreign trust files Form 3520-A and furnishes the required annual statements to its US owners and US beneficiaries. The return is due by the fifteenth day of the third month after the end of the trust's tax year. Thus, for a calendar-year taxpayer, the return is due by March 15.

Because the IRS has no jurisdiction (power) over the foreign trust (but does have jurisdiction over the US settlor of the trust), the US tax law provides that the US owner is subject to an initial penalty equal to the **greater of** $10,000 or 5 percent of the gross value of the portion of the trust's assets, treated as owned by the US person at the close of that tax year, if the foreign trust (a) fails to file a timely Form 3520-A or (b) does not furnish all of the information required by the tax law or includes incorrect information.

Additional penalties will be imposed if the noncompliance continues after the IRS mails a notice of failure to comply with the required reporting.

Criminal penalties may also be imposed for failure to file on time and for filing a false or fraudulent return.

All of the above potential problems can be avoided by hiring competent professionals to implement and maintain your planning.

 c. <u>Form 1040NR.</u>

Form 1040NR is the US income tax return for the foreign trust while the settlor is living. The trust will pay no US (or other) income tax while the settlor is living, because it is a grantor trust as discussed above. The Form 1040NR is informational in nature and is used to notify the IRS of the trust's income, deductions and credits that will be reported on the income tax return of the US settlor. The return is due by the fifteenth day of the sixth month after the end of the tax year (June 15 for calendar-year taxpayers).

 2. <u>Foreign Account & Foreign Asset Reporting</u>

If either your client or your client's trust is the owner of (or has signature or other authority over) a foreign bank, securities, or other financial account, additional reporting may be required as an attachment to your client's income tax return on IRS Form 8938 (Form 8938 is also used to report other foreign assets) and, separately, on Fincen Form 114, Report of Foreign Bank and Financial Accounts (*note:* >>>Fincen Form 114 can only be filed electronically; one may do so at: https://bsaefiling1.fincen.treas.gov/noregfilerupload <<<), and your client may have to check the box on Schedule B Part III, line 7 of his/her Form 1040 (or other US income tax form) to report the existence of the account. Note: significant penalties may be imposed for the late filing or failure to file these forms.

CHAPTER X

IRS SCRUTINY OF ABUSIVE TRUST ARRANGEMENTS

A. Definition of Abusive Trust.

Abusive trust arrangements are typically promoted by the promise of tax benefits with no meaningful change in the settlor's control over or benefit from the settlor's income or assets. The most commonly promised benefits include
- reduction or elimination of income subject to tax;
- deductions for personal expenses paid by the trust;
- depreciation deductions for an owner's personal residence and furnishings;
- a stepped-up basis for property transferred to the trust;
- the reduction or elimination of self-employment taxes; and
- the reduction or elimination of gift and estate taxes.
- These promised benefits are inconsistent with the tax rules applicable to trusts and the other entities that may also be involved.

B. IRS Examples of Abusive Trust Arrangements

The schemes targeted by the Internal Revenue Service (the "Service") often consist of convoluted, multi-tiered structures, typically involving more than one trust (and other entities as well), each holding different assets of the taxpayer (for example, the taxpayer's business might be owned by one entity, the business equipment by a second entity, the taxpayer's home by a third, and an automobile by a fourth), as well as interests in other trusts. Funds may flow from one trust to another trust by way of rental agreements, fees for services, purchase and sale agreements, and distributions. Some trusts purport to involve charitable purposes. In some situations, one or more foreign trusts may also be part of the arrangement. In Notice 97-24,[267] the Service classified abusive trust arrangements into the following five types and further indicated that an abusive arrangement might involve some or all of the arrangements described below.

1. The Business Trust

This scheme involves the transfer of a business by its owner to a "trust" (sometimes described as an unincorporated business trust) in exchange for ownership or beneficial interest certificates. The trust makes payments to the holders of these certificates, deducting such payments as either a business expense or a trust distribution, which purports to result in the reduction of the taxable income of the business. Of course, the owner's self-employment income is eliminated because he is receiving "distributions from a trust," not income from self-employment. In some cases, the connivance purports to eliminate the owner's estate tax liability through a "self-canceling at death" feature of the trust units (alternatively, by a sale at a nominal price).

2. The Equipment or Service Trust

The equipment trust is formed to hold equipment that is rented or leased to the business trust, often at inflated rates. The service trust is formed to provide services to the business trust, often for inflated fees. Under these abusive trust arrangements, income is drained from the business trust through inflated rentals or fees, and those amounts are offset by the equipment trust through inflated depreciation deductions resulting from a sham "purchase" of the equipment by the trust. In addition, distorting a long-established tax law principle,[268] the owner ("seller" of the equipment) takes the inconsistent position that the trust units he received in exchange for the sale of the equipment had an indeterminable value, and that he therefore owes no tax on the sale. Both the equipment and the service trust will often utilize distributions to other trusts to further reduce or eliminate trust income.

3. The Family Residence Trust

The owner of the family residence transfers the residence, including its furnishings, to a trust. The goal of this arrangement is to convert nondeductible personal expenditures into "deductible" items. The machinations created to effect the desired result again include the taking of inconsistent positions by the trust and the owner: the trust takes the position that it has acquired the residence in an exchange that resulted in a stepped-up basis, with respect to which the trust is allowed a depreciation deduction because it is in the "business" of renting the property; little or no rent is paid, of course, and the owner takes the position that no gain is recognized on the sale because the trust units he received have no ascertainable value (again based on a distortion of a long and well-established tax law principle[269]), and he and his family can live rent-free in the residence as its caretakers (for the benefit of the trust). In the event the trust were to receive income, it would be offset by depreciation deductions on the "rental" property held by the trust.

4. The Charitable Trust

This scheme involves the use of a charitable trust to pay for the personal educational, living, or recreational expenses of the owner or the owner's family. For example, the trust may provide for payments to the University of Miami (an otherwise deductible educational gift), and such payments will in fact be utilized for the college tuition of a child of the owner.

5. The Final Trust

In some multitrust arrangements, the US owner of one or more abusive trusts establishes a trust (the "final trust") that holds trust units of the owner's other trusts and is the final distributee of their income. A final trust often is formed in a foreign country that imposes little or no tax on the trust.

A common factor in each of these trusts is that the original owner of the assets that are nominally subject to the trust effectively retains authority to cause the financial benefits of the trust to be directly or indirectly returned or made available to the owner. For example, the trustee may be the promoter, or a relative or friend of the owner, who simply carries out the directions of the owner whether or not permitted by the terms of the trust. Often, the trustee gives the owner checks that are presigned by the trustee, checks that are accompanied by a rubber stamp of the trustee's signature, a credit card, or a debit card with the intention of permitting the owner to obtain cash from the trust or otherwise to use the assets of the trust for the owner's benefit.

Note: recall that the asset protection trust does not provide any income tax benefit.

CHAPTER XI

HOW TO SELECT AN ASSET PROTECTION ATTORNEY

Selecting an asset protection attorney can be a daunting task, especially when so many inexperienced attorneys advertise asset protection services. So how can one weed out the bad from the good—the unqualified from the qualified? We have developed this list of twelve questions that should be asked of every asset protection attorney before he or she is retained for your client or works with you for your client.

(1) *How long have you been implementing asset protection plans?*

Too often an attorney will advertise the number of years he has been admitted to practice law. This can be deceiving, as the attorney may have recently switched his/her area of practice. Instead, ask how long he/she has been practicing in the area of asset protection. See if he/she can point you to articles or publications that show his or her years of experience in this specific area.

(2) *Will your firm provide federal tax compliance guidance?*

Offshore asset protection requires broad knowledge of tax law. Look for a firm with extensive experience in tax. Ask if the firm will guide your CPA in preparing the necessary tax returns.

(3) *How many asset protection structures have you implemented?*

The answer you are looking for is "hundreds." Think of asset protection like complex surgery. If you needed open-heart surgery, you would want the surgeon who has successfully performed the procedure hundreds of times.

(4) *What portion of your practice is dedicated to asset protection planning?*

Many estate planning attorneys purport to practice asset protection planning, but inquiry reveals that 90 percent of their practice is devoted to other matters. You want the attorney that does offshore asset protection all day, every day—100 percent.

(5) *What is your rate of success?*

Anything less than 100 percent should have you concerned. Why did the creditor reach the client's assets if the structure was implemented properly?

(6) *Can you point me to third parties who can recommend your services?*

Attorneys who focus their practice in offshore asset protection work with trust companies, protector companies, financial advisors, and perhaps CPAs, to properly implement the structure. Ask for the contact information for some of those third party professionals, and see if they recommend the attorney. Ask the third party how much experience the attorney has in the field and how many structures he has implemented with them.

(7) *Does your practice represent creditors?*

An attorney may focus his or her practice in asset protection structures but primarily represent the creditors seeking to bust up the structures. Make sure the attorney's experience and successes are in implementing structures, not representing creditors or only acting as an expert witness.

(8) *What type of due diligence have you conducted on the offshore trustee?*

Many attorneys select offshore trustees, protectors, and banks based solely on marketing materials or trade shows. Verify that the attorney has personally met with the trustee, protector, and banks by visiting their foreign offices (and ask how frequently). Ask about the offshore providers' track record, stability, and managing personnel. If the attorney is not intimately familiar with these companies, you should be concerned.

(9) *Are you an AV Preeminent®[270] rated attorney?*

Martindale-Hubbell, the nationwide lawyer information organization, facilitates an attorney peer-rating program that measures the attorney's level of professionalism and ethics. The highest possible rating is AV Preeminent®.

(10) *Have you authored any materials on asset protection that were published by reputable* legal publishers?

In the days of the internet and self-publishing, many attorneys now call themselves "authors." The true test is whether reputable legal publishers have selected the attorney to write on asset protection planning in reference materials used by attorneys, CPAs and other professionals.

(11) *Have you been an expert speaker, a guest lecturer at an educational institution, or a professor on the subject of asset protection?*

Attorneys respected in the field of asset protection will have been asked to conduct seminars for bar associations or other professional organizations, will have been guest lecturers at educational institutions, and may have served as professors or adjunct professors at law schools.

How To Select An Asset Protection Attorney

(12) Can you tell me the total cost of implementation during my initial consultation?

Unlike litigation, the time and costs associated with implementing an asset protection structure are foreseeable for an experienced asset protection attorney and therefore should be determined before the lawyer is retained. Be sure the price quoted includes all legal fees and costs of implementation (such as trustee and protector fees). Ask if the fee includes continuing consultations so your client can have questions answered, or will your client be charged at an hourly rate to ask a question? Price can be an important factor, but the success of the planning should be most important. Any amount spent is an amount potentially wasted if your client fails to pick the right attorney.

ENDNOTES

[1] For example, coauthor Howard Rosen appeared on the April 2, 2014, *Daily Show with Jon Stewart* in a segment on the Cook Islands.

[2] Versus business or entity asset protection planning, discussed later.

[3] See section XI for guidance in selecting a competent attorney.

[4] "Future potential creditor" is a term of art referring to the unknown creditor—the creditor with whom you have not yet done (or contemplated doing) business at the time of the transfer. *See, e.g., Oberst v. Oberst*, 91 B.R. 97 (D.C. Cal. 1988), where the court distinguished between transfers prompted by a desire to place property beyond the reach of potential future creditors and transfers intended to defraud creditors entitled to protection under applicable fraudulent transfer laws. *See also Hurlbert v. Shackleton*, 560 So.2d 1276 (Fla. 1st Dist. 1990), where the dissent distinguished between "probable" and "possible" future creditors, the former being entitled to fraudulent transfer law protection, while the latter were not so entitled.

[5] The word "true" in this text is used to distinguish real gifts from secret asset return arrangements discussed in I B 4.

[6] The person to whom a gift is made.

[7] The gift tax consequences of an outright gift are distinguishable

based upon the identity of the donee: generally, gifts to a US citizen spouse will qualify for the unlimited federal gift tax marital deduction, while gifts to nonspouse donees and to non-US citizen spouses will only be eligible for the federal gift tax annual exclusion. § 2523(a), § 2523 (i). Note: Section (§) references are to sections of the US Internal Revenue Code of 1986, and the Internal Revenue Service regulations unless otherwise noted or required by the context.

[8] The person who makes a gift.

[9] Although even the interest of a nonsettlor beneficiary of a testamentary trust may be exposed. In an unexpected interpretation of the term "similar device" a bankruptcy court so held: *See In re Castellano,* 2014 WL 3881338 (Bk.N.D.Ill., Aug. 6, 2014).

[10] The term "transferor" includes a settlor (a person who creates a trust) and a donor (a person who makes a gift).

[11] *But see In re Castellano,* 2014 WL 3881338 (Bk.N.D.Ill., Aug. 6, 2014).

[12] The common-law tenancy by the entireties was characterized by five coincident unities: unity of possession (joint ownership and control), unity of interest (the interests must be the same), unity of title (the interests must originate in the same instrument), unity of time (the interests must commence simultaneously), and the unity of marriage. The unity of possession required the husband and wife to act together to convey title to tenancy by the entireties property, precluding unilateral severance (transfer or encumbrance).

Endnotes

[13] *See, e.g., First National Bank of Leesburg v. Hector Supply Company,* 254 So.2d 777 (Fla. 1971); *Maryland National Bank v. Pearce,* 620 A.2d 941 (Md. App. 1993); *Barker Brothers, Inc. v. Barker-Taylor,* 823 P.2d 1204 (Wyo. 1992). Even where the "creditor" is the United States in a criminal forfeiture proceeding. *US v. One Single Family Residence With Out Buildings Located At 15621 S.W. 209 Avenue, Miami, Florida,* 894 F.2d 1511 (11th Cir. 1990).

[14] § 2523(a). The unlimited marital deduction is not available if the donee spouse is not a US citizen, or if the transferred interest is a nondeductible terminable interest, § 2523(i),(b).

[15] *See Sharp v. Hamilton,* 520 So.2d 9 (Fla. 1988), affirming 495 So.2d 235 (Fla. 5th DCA 1986); *Constitution Bank v. Olsen,* 620 A.2d 1146 (Superior Ct. Pa. 1993).

[16] A body of English law that originated with an oral tradition of tribal justice in Britain thousands of years ago and developed into a unique, cohesive body of law set to writing by English judges over time, which was eventually imported as the law of British colonies throughout the world such as the United States of America (except Louisiana), Canada (except Quebec), and India. Statute law started the gradual replacement of much of the common law, but not before England had begun to colonize the world. Many jurisdictions began their legal system with whatever the state of the law was at the time their colony was established, thereby perpetuating their union with the British common-law system.

[17] *Klajbor v. Klajbor,* 94 N.E.2d 502 (Ill. 1950).

[18] Under common law, each joint tenant was the owner of the undivided whole of the property. *Kane v. Johnson,* 73 N.E.2d 321 (Ill. 1947). However, the creditor of a joint tenant can only reach that tenant's fractional interest in the property.

[19] Reg. § 25.2511-1(h)(4) and (5). § 2523.

[20] *Park Enterprises, Inc. v. Trach,* 47 N.W.2d 194 (Minn. 1951); *but see Union Properties, Inc. v. Cleveland Trust Co,* 89 N.E.2d 638 (Ohio 1949).

[21] *See Klajbor v. Klajbor,* 94 N.E.2d 502 (Ill. 1950).

[22] The origin, history, and purpose of this type of business organization was described by the New York Court in *Ames v. Downing,* 1 Bradf. 321 (1850), 329–330: "The system of limited partnerships, which was introduced by statute into this State, and subsequently very generally adopted in many other States of the Union, was borrowed from the French Code. (3 Kent, 36; Code de Commerce, 19, 23, 24.) Under the name of La Société en commandite, it has existed in France from the time of the middle ages; mention being made of it in the most ancient commercial records, and in the early mercantile regulations of Marseilles and Montpelier. In the vulgar Latinity of the Middle Ages it was styled Commenda, and in Italy Accomenda. In the statutes of Pisa and Florence, it is recognized so far back as the year 1160; also in the ordinance of Louis-le-Hutin, 1315; the statutes of Marseilles, 1253; of Geneva, 1588. In the Middle Ages, it was one of the most frequent combinations of trade and was the basis of the active and widely extended commerce of the opulent maritime cities of Italy. It contributed largely

to the support of the great and prosperous trade carried on along the shores of the Mediterranean, was known in Languedoc, Provence, and Lombardy, entered into most of the industrial occupations and pursuits of the age, and even travelled under the protection of the arms of the Crusaders to the city of Jerusalem. At a period when capital was in the hands of nobles and clergy, who, from pride of caste, or canonical regulations, could not engage directly in trade, it afforded the means of secretly embarking on commercial enterprises and reaping the profits of such lucrative pursuits without personal risk; and thus the vast wealth, which otherwise would have lain dormant in the coffers of the rich, became the foundation, by means of this ingenious idea, of that great commerce which made princes of the merchants, elevated the trading classes, and brought the Commons into position as an influential estate in the common wealth."

[23] Alabama, Arkansas, California, District of Columbia, Florida, Hawaii, Idaho, Illinois, Iowa, Kentucky, Maine, Minnesota, Montana, Nevada, New Mexico, North Dakota, Oklahoma, Utah, Washington.

[24] ULPA §§ 404; 303 (2001). No partner, not even a general partner, is liable for the "inside" debts of a limited liability limited partnership (LLLP).

[25] ULPA § 303 (2001).

[26] Id.

[27] A judgment creditor is a person who holds a judgment against another person, the judgment debtor.

[28] A partner's interest in a limited partnership is personal property. ULPA § 701 (2001). A partner in a limited partnership has no rights to specific partnership property that is reachable by his creditor.

[29] ULPA § 703(b) (2001).

[30] *See, Bank of Bethesda v. Koch*, 408 A.2d 767 (Md. App. 1979).

[31] ULPA § 703(e) (2001). *Chrysler Credit Corp. v. Peterson*, 342 N.W.2d 170 (Minn. App. 1984); *In re Stocks*, 110 B.R. 65 (N.D. Fla. 1989).

[32] *See,* ULPA § 702 (2001).

[33] 1977-1 C.B. 178.

[34] § 721; Regs. § 1.721-1(a).

[35] § 721(b).

[36] § 702(a).

[37] Particularly in those states where such a payment might qualify for a wage exemption. *See, e.g.,* Fla. Stat. § 222.11.

[38] § 707(c). The ultimate deductibility by the partner of the allocated expense may be limited by US tax law.

[39] *See* PLR 9310039; PLR 9131006. Assuming that the recipient spouse is a US citizen. *See,* § 2523(i).

Endnotes

[40] PLR 9131006; §§ 2501, 2503.

[41] *See*, Rev. Rul. 93-12, 1993-7 I.R.B. 13 for the left-handed indication by the service that such discounts may be available.

[42] *See Estate of Christofani v. Comm'r*, 97 T.C. 74 (1991); Treas. Reg. § 25.2503-3(a); and Rev. Rul. 81-7, 1981-1 C.B. 474.

[43] *See* Treas. Reg. § 25.2511-2(c),(j). *See also*, Section IX, below.

[44] Such as Nevis and the Cook Islands.

[45] *See, e.g.,* for a state enacting a foreign LLC statute, but not a domestic LLC statute: Ind. Code § 23-16-10.1-1.

[46] In this context "disregarded" means that the LLC is treated as if it does not exist for US income tax purposes. See IRS Form 8832 which permits certain entities to make an election to be disregarded.

[47] The tax owner of a disregarded entity is the person that is treated as owning the assets and liabilities of the disregarded entity for purposes of US income tax law.

[48] A judge would simply order the settlor to revoke the trust and pay his creditor.

[49] *Van Stewart v. Townsend*, 28 P.2d 999 (Wash. 1934); *Schofield v. Cleveland Trust Co.*, 21 N.E.2d 119 (Ohio 1939).

[50] *See Matter of Estate of Kovalyshyn*, 343 A.2d 852 (NJ Super. 1975) where the court held that even though a retained power of revocation did not invalidate the trust, the trust assets would, because of such retained power, be available to satisfy the settlor's debts; *Johnson v. Commercial Bank*, 588 P.2d 1096 (Ore. 1978), where the court held that the power of revocation was tantamount to a general power of appointment, thus making the trust assets available to satisfy the claims of the settlor's creditors. *See also* 11 USC § 541(a)(1). *But see Creditors' Rights Against Trust Assets*, 22 Real Prop., Prob. and Trust J. 735, at p. 738, and fn's 15 and 16 thereat (Winter 1987).

[51] Fla. Stat. § 733.707(3). *See In Re Granwell*, 228 N.E.2d 779 (NY 1967); *State Street Bank & Trust Co. v. Reiser*, 389 N.E.2d 768 (Mass.App.Ct. 1979); *Matter of Estate of Kovalyshyn*, 343 A.2d 852 (N.J. Super. 1975). *See also* 5 *American Law of Property* § 23.18 (Casner Ed. 1952); 4 *Scott on Trusts* § 330.12.

[52] *But see In re Castellano*, 2014 WL 3881338 (Bk.N.D.Ill., Aug. 6, 2014).

[53] Restatement (Second) of Trusts § 155 (1959); see also 11 USC § 541(c)(2).

[54] *Pemberton v. Pemberton*, 411 N.E.2d 1305 (Mass.App. 1980), "...the settlor's intent to deny creditors of a beneficiary recovery against trust assets or recovery against the trustee's wishes has been accorded particular deference, even in the face of strong public policy arguments favoring...recovery." at 1312. See also *Town of Randolph v. Roberts*, 195 N.E.2d 72 (Mass. 1964). Note, however, that if the

beneficiary has been granted significant rights to deal with trust property, the protection otherwise afforded by the discretionary or other spendthrift provision may be rendered ineffective. *Cf., In Re Threewitt*, 20 B.R. 434 (D. Kan. 1982), *rev'd*, 24 B.R. 927 (D. Kan. 1982).

[55] *See generally Creditors' Rights Against Trust Assets*, 22 Real Prop., Prob. and Trust J. 735 (Winter, 1987).

[56] *Ware v. Gulda*, 117 N.E.2d 137 (Mass. 1954); *See also* Restatement (Second) of Trusts § 156(2) comment e (1957).

[57] Restatement (Second) of Trusts § 156, comment d (1957).

[58] Restatement (Second) of Trusts § 156(1) (1957). *But see* Mo. Stat. § 456.080(3).

[59] No specific language is required to create a spendthrift trust - a statement in the trust to the effect that it is a spendthrift trust will be sufficient. Restatement, supra, § 152, comment c. *See also* Nev. Rev. Stat. § 166.050.

[60] 11 USC § 541(c)(2). Some states have enacted statutes specifically providing this result. *See*, Ariz. Rev. Stat. §§ 14-7701, 14-7702; Del. Stat. § 3536; Ind. Stat. § 30-4-3-2; Ky. Stat. § 381.180; La. Rev. Stat. § 9:2002; Nev. Stat. § 21.080(2); N.M. Stat. § 42-9-4 (1978); Ga. Stat. § 53-12-28; Okla. Stat. tit. 60, § 175.25; R.I.Stat. 1956 § 18-9.1-1 (1988); Tex. Prop. Code § 112.035; W. Va. Stat. 1966 § 36-1-18. However, in some states an interest in an otherwise valid spendthrift trust will be

available to provide for a beneficiary's spouse and children. *See, e.g., Bacardi v. White*, 463 So.2d 218 (Fla. 1985); *Matt v. Matt*, 473 N.E.2d 1310 (Ill. 1985); Cal. Prob. Code § 15305.

[61] Restatement (Second) of Trusts § 156(1) (1957).

[62] *DiMaria v. Bank of California National Association*, 237 Cal. App.2d 254, 46 Cal. Rptr. 924 (1st DCA 1965). *See also, Avera v. Avera*, 315 S.E.2d 883 (Ga. 1984), holding for settlor-beneficiary as to trust principal, which the trustee could only distribute to the settlor under circumstances of "misfortune, illness, accident, or infirmity" and for necessary sums when there were no other "funds reasonably available."

[63] Alaska: Alaska Stat. § 34.40.110 (1997); Colorado: Colo. Rev. Stat. § 38-10-111 (2001); Delaware: Del. Code Ann. tit. 12, §§ 3570-3576 (1997); Hawaii: H.R.S. 554G (2011); Missouri: Mo. Rev. Stat. § 456.5-505 (1989); Nevada: Nev. Rev. Stat. § 166.010-166.170 (1999); New Hampshire: N.H. Rev. Stat. Ann. § 564-D:1-18 (2009); Oklahoma: Okla. Stat. tit. 31 § 11, *et seq.* (2004); Rhode Island: RI Gen. Laws § 18-9.2-1, *et seq.* (1999); South Dakota: SDCL §§ 55-16-1 to 55-16-16 (2005); Tennessee: Tenn. Code Ann. § 35-16-101 (2007); Utah: Utah Code Ann. § 25-6-14 (2003); Virginia: Virginia Code §§ 55-545.03:2 and 55-545.03:3 (2012); Wyoming: Wyo. Stat. §§ 4-1-505 and 4-10-510-523 (2007), Ohio: Ohio Laws Ch. 5816 (2013).

[64] *See, e.g., DiMaria v. Bank of California National Association*, 237 Cal. App.2d 254, 46 Cal. Rptr. 924 (1st DCA 1965).

[65] *See, e.g., In Re Estate of Strauss*, 347 N.Y.S.2d 840 (1973), where the trust was not recognized with respect to real property situated in Germany. See also *William F. Buckley v. Comm'r*, 22 T.C. 1312 (1954), *aff'd per curiam*, 231 F.2d 204 (2d Cir. 1956), Venezuela did not recognize trust concept, entity was classified as a corporation with no pass-through of deductions; *In Re Tabbagh's Estate*, 3 N.Y.S.2d 542 (1938), trusts not recognized in France.

[66] Civil law-based regarding property interests and inheritance.

[67] *See, e.g., Estate of Oei T. Swan v. Comm'r*, 24 T.C. 829 (1955), *rev'd in part & aff'd in part*, 247 F.2d 144 (2d Cir.1957), where *Stiftungs* established in Liechtenstein and Switzerland were treated as revocable trusts, despite the holding in *Aramo-Stiftung v. Comm'r*, 172 F.2d 896 (2d Cir. 1949), *aff'g as modified*, 9 T.C. 947 (1947), defining *Stiftungs* as entities similar to corporations.

[68] 13 Elizabeth I Ch. 5 (1571).

[69] Except possibly in a bankruptcy context.

[70] *See, e.g.*, International Trusts Amendment Act 1991, No. 32, § 6 (Cook Islands), which provides: "The enactment titled 13 Elizabeth I Ch 5 (1571) shall have no application to any settlement upon or disposition to an international trust."

[71] *See, e.g.*, Fraudulent Dispositions Act, 1991 § 3 (The Bahamas); Fraudulent Dispositions Law, 1989 § 3 (Cayman Islands).

[72] *See, e.g.,* Fraudulent Dispositions Law, 1989 § 4 (Cayman Islands), providing a six-year statute of limitations, and § 2 thereof which defines the terms "creditor" and "obligation" for purposes of the law; Fraudulent Dispositions Act, 1991 § 4 (The Bahamas), providing a two-year statute of limitations, and § 2 thereof which, *inter alia*, defines an "obligation" as an obligation or liability (including a contingent liability) which existed on the date of the transfer, and of which the transferor had *actual notice*; International Trusts Act 1984 § 13B (Cook Islands), providing a two-year statute; Bankruptcy (Amendment) Ordinance, 1990, § 42A (Gibraltar), which provides that if the settlor is an individual and is not insolvent at the date of the transfer, is not rendered insolvent by the transfer, and registers the transfer, then no creditor - existing or subsequent - can set aside the transfer. For purposes of determining solvency under this provision, the settlor's contingent liabilities of which he had *actual knowledge* are taken into account. *See also* § 61 of Trusts Ordinance 1990 (Turks and Caicos Islands).

[73] International Trusts Act 1984 § 13B (Cook Islands), utilizes the standard of proof required in the United States to convict a person of a capital offense, by stating: "Where it is proven *beyond reasonable doubt* by a creditor..." (emphasis added).

[74] Because any US court finding that a fraudulent transfer had occurred would be ignored in the Cook Islands.

[75] Although retaining a power of revocation is generally not recommended in an APT.

[76] *See also* International Trusts Act 1984 § 13F (Cook Islands).

[77] *See also* International Trusts Law 1992 § 12 (Cyprus); International Trusts Act 1984 § 21 (Cook Islands).

[78] *See, e.g., US v. Levine*, 951 F.2d 1466 (6th Cr. 1991), a criminal case where pressure was exerted on the US branch of a Swiss bank to release information.

[79] *Federal Trade Commission v. Affordable Media, LLC*, 179 F.3d 1228 (9th Cir. 1999), popularly referred to as the Anderson case.

[80] *Lawrence v. Goldberg*, 279 F. 3d 1294 (11th Cir. 2002); *Lawrence v. Goldberg*, 244 B.R. 868 (S.D. Fla. 2000); *In Re Lawrence*, 235 B.R. 498 (Bankr. S.D. Fla. 1999); *Goldberg v. Lawrence*, 227 B.R. 907 (Bankr. S.D. Fla. 1998).

[81] 333 US 56 (1948).

[82] 460 US 752 (1983). *See also, US v. Bryan*, 339 US 323 (1950).

[83] 2014 WL 1603759 (S.D. Fla. 2014). Only the Westlaw citation was available at the time this was written.

[84] 333 US 56 (1948).

[85] *Federal Trade Commission v. Affordable Media, LLC*, 179 F.3d 1228 (9th Cir. 1999).

[86] See section IV A 2 iv, below.

[87] *Lawrence v. Goldberg*, 279 F. 3d 1294 (11 th Cir. 2002).

[88] Treas. Reg. § 301.7701-4(a).

[89] *See, e.g., Comm'r v. Guitar Trust Estate*, 72 F.2d 544 (5th Cir. 1934); *Elmstreet Realty Trust v. Comm'r*, 76 T.C. 803 (1981), acq., 1981-2 C.B. 1. *But see* Rev. Rul. 75-258, 1975-2 C.B. 503, finding an association taxable as a corporation.

[90] *See* Treas. Reg. § 301.7701(c). If the arrangement is not treated as a trust, it will be treated as an association taxable as a corporation.

[91] *See, e.g.,* Rev. Rul. 73-100, 1973-1 C.B. 613.

[92] *See* IV B 1 b i, above for the definition of an offshore trust for purposes of this book.

[93] Effective for taxable years beginning after 1996 unless the trustee irrevocably elects to apply same to tax years ending after the date of enactment of August 20, 1996. P.L. 104-188, § 1907(a).

[94] *See* Treas. Reg. § 301.7701-7(1)(a)(i).

[95] *See* Treas. Reg. § 301.7701-7(1)(a)(ii).

[96] § 1361(c)(2)(A). A "grantor trust" is a trust which, for federal income tax purposes, is treated as "owned" by the settlor of the trust

under Subpart E of Part I of Subchapter J of Chapter 1 of Subtitle A of the Internal Revenue Code (§§ 671-679). As the "owner" of the trust, § 671 requires the settlor to report the income, deductions, and credits of the owned portion of the trust on his or her tax return.

[97] § 684(a).

[98] A tax-law-created fiction. Under trust law, no one "owns" a trust.

[99] Such as utilizing one's federal gift tax lifetime exemption and excluding future appreciation from federal estate taxation. The authors call such a trust an "estate freeze" trust.

[100] *See, e.g., Sanford v. Comm'r*, 308 US 39 (1939).

[101] For this purpose, a special power of appointment is one under which the power holder may appoint (direct the distribution of) subject property to anyone other than to himself or herself, his or her estate, or the creditors of either. In the APT context, it is also advisable to preclude a settlor from making an outright appointment to his or her spouse, since it is possible that both could be liable to a creditor.

[102] Treas. Reg. § 25.2511-2(f). Such gifts may or may not be reportable, depending upon their qualification for the § 2503(b) annual exclusion, the § 2503(c) exclusion for medical/educational expenses. Such distributions, made within three years of the settlor's death, even though excluded as gifts, may be brought back into the settlor's estate under the authority of *Estate of Jalkut v. Comm'r*, 96 T.C. 675 (1991), acq., 1991-2 C.B. 1. *See also* Tech. Adv. Mem. 9139002 (June 14, 1991).

[103] § 2033.

[104] § 2010.

[105] § 2056.

[106] § 2601 et seq.

[107] Be very careful modifying a marital deduction provision; the last thing you want to do is lose a marital deduction.

[108] This section was prepared for inclusion in this book by Jeffrey M. Verdon, an attorney in Newport Beach, California, whose law practice is concentrated in asset protection planning and estate planning.

[109] § 1014(b)(6).

[110] Restatement (Second) of Trusts § 187 (1957). *But see* Id., § 156, for limitation on protection where the settlor is the beneficiary. *See also* discussion in Section IV A 1 a ii, above, relating to domestic discretionary trusts.

[111] *See* Restatement (Second) of Trusts § 155, comment c (1957).

[112] A court may consider some or all of the following factors in determining whether an abuse of discretion has occurred: (1) the extent of the discretion conferred upon the trustee by the terms of the trust; (2) the purposes of the trust; (3) the nature of the power;

(4) the existence or nonexistence, the definiteness or indefiniteness, of an external standard by which the reasonableness of the trustee's conduct can be judged; (5) the motives of the trustee in exercising or refraining from exercising the power; (6) the existence or nonexistence of an interest in the trustee conflicting with that of the beneficiaries. Language in the trust to the effect that it is the settlor's intent that the trustee exercise its discretion in such a manner as to maximize the preservation of trust assets can aid in mitigating an abuse of discretion argument.

[113] Restatement (Second) of Trusts § 152, comment c (1957).

[114] *Domo v. McCarthy*, 612 N.E.2d 706 (Ohio 1993); *Scott v. Bank One Trust Company*, 577 N.E.2d 1077 (Ohio 1991).

[115] Restatement (Second) of Trusts § 150, Illust. 1 (1957).

[116] *See, e.g.,* 11 USC § 541(c)(2); Ariz. Stat. § 14-7706; Cal. Prob. Code § 15301(a); 12 Del. Code § 3536(a); Ga. Stat. § 53-12-28(b). *See also* discussion in Section IV A 1 a ii, above, relating to domestic spendthrift trusts, and the ineffectiveness of the provision with respect to a settlor-beneficiary.

[117] For example, the trust instrument may permit the trustee to require a statement sworn under oath by the person exercising the power to the effect that the power is being exercised of that person's own free will.

[118] The governing law to which the trust is subject must, of course,

permit the existence of such powers over the trustees without causing the trust to be treated as a sham.

[119] *US v. Rylander*, 460 US 752 (1983); *US v. Bryan*, 339 US 323 (1950).

[120] Such a mechanism might be a power of attorney granted to the protector in the trust instrument to change signatories on financial accounts of the trust to a successor trustee, or it could be a direction in the trust instrument to any custodian financial institution (which institution would customarily have an original of the trust document) to follow the directions of the protector in changing the account signatories to a successor trustee. Such a mechanism can obviate the need for current trustee participation in effecting such changes, which can be important if the current trustee is under some type of restraint that would preclude such participation.

[121] *See also* International Trust Law 1992, § 9 (Cyprus); International Trusts Act 1984, § 13G(4) (Cook Islands); Trust (Foreign Element) Law, 1987, § 4(4) (Cayman Islands).

[122] *See also* International Trust Act 1984, § 2 (Cook Islands), which defines the term "protector" for purposes of the Act.

[123] Section 50 of the Trustees Act 1956 (New Zealand) provides for the utilization of custodian trustees, and is applicable in the Cook Islands.

[124] See section IX.

[125] Id.

[126] 13 Elizabeth I Ch. 5 (1571). As an example of the influence of the Statute of Elizabeth on, as an example, Florida's original fraudulent conveyance statute, here is how that law read in 1823 when first enacted in Florida:

> Every feoffment, gift, grant, alienation, bargain, sale, conveyance, transfer and assignment of lands, tenements, hereditaments, and of goods and chattels, or any of them, or any lease, rent, use, common or other profit, benefit or charge whatever out of lands, tenements, hereditaments or goods and chattels, or any of them, by writing or otherwise, and every bond, note, contract, suit, judgment and execution which shall at any time hereafter be had, made or executed, contrived or devised of fraud, covin, collusion or guile, to the end, purpose or intent to delay, hinder or defraud creditors or others of their just and lawful actions, suits, debts, accounts, damages, demands, penalties or forfeitures, shall be from henceforth as against the person or persons, or bodies politic or corporate, his, her or their successors, executors, administrators and assigns, and every one of them so intended to be delayed, hindered or defrauded, deemed, held, adjudged and taken to be utterly void, frustrate and of none effect, any pretense, color, feigned consideration, expressing of use or any other matter or thing to the contrary notwithstanding; provided, that this section, or

anything therein contained, shall not extend to any estate or interest in lands, tenements, hereditaments, leases, rents, uses, commons, profits, goods or chattels which shall be had, made, conveyed or assured if such estate shall be, upon good consideration and bona fide, lawfully conveyed or assured to any person or persons, or body politic or corporate, not having at the time of such conveyance or assurance to them made any manner of notice or knowledge of such covin, fraud or collusion as aforesaid, anything in this section to the contrary notwithstanding.

[127] 11 USC § 548.

[128] Uniform Fraudulent Transfer Act 1984 § 4(a)(1) (UFTA). The various fraudulent transfer statutes also refer to "obligations incurred" by a debtor; however, for enhanced readability, the text only refers to transfers.

[129] Id., § 4(a)(2).

[130] 11 U.S.C § 548.

[131] UFTA § 5(a).

[132] UFTA § 2(b).

[133] "Property" being further defined in § 1(10) to mean anything that may be the subject of ownership.

[134] UFTA § 2(d).

[135] UFTA § 1(5).

[136] UFTA § 1(3).

[137] *See In Re Xonics Photochemical*, 841 F.2d 198 (7th Cir. 1988).

[138] UFTA § 2(e).

[139] A's homestead and related debt are taken out of the computation; thus, since his countable assets and debts are equal, a gratuitous transfer of even one dollar would render A insolvent.

[140] *Dean v. Heimbach*, 409 So.2d 157 (Fla. 1st Dist. 1982); *Sneed v. Davis*, 184 So. 865 (Fla. 1938).

[141] As long as the creditor took action within the relevant statute of limitations. *See* UFTA § 9 (statute of limitations).

[142] 560 So.2d 1276 (Fla. 1st Dist. 1990).

[143] Id.

[144] 91 B.R. 97 (C.D. Cal. 1988).

[145] 112 N.Y.S.2d 546 (1952).

[146] Id. at 548.

[147] 214 P.2d 477 (Wyo. 1950).

[148] Id, at 483.

[149] *Twyne's Case*, 3 Coke 80b, 76 Eng. Rep. 809 (Star Chamber 1601).

[150] 13 Elizabeth I Ch. 5 (1571).

[151] Uniform Fraudulent Conveyance Act 1918 § 7.

[152] UFTA § 4, Comment 5.

[153] *See, e.g., Rosenberg v. Aarnel Funding Corp.*, 575 So.2d 753 (Fla. 3d Dist. 1991); *Emerson v. Opp*, 38 N.E. 330 (Ind. 1894).

[154] UFTA § 5(a).

[155] UFTA § 4(a)(2).

[156] *See, e.g., Service Finance Corp. v. Werber*, 564 N.Y.S.2d 408 (1st Dept. 1991).

[157] UFTA § 7.

[158] Id.

[159] *See, e.g., Grupo Mexicano De Desarrollo, SA, et al., v. Alliance Bond Fund, Inc., et al.*, 527 US 308 (1999); *Martin v. James B. Berry Sons' Co.*, 83 F.2d 857 (1st Cir. 1936).

Endnotes

[160] *Republic of the Philippines v. Marcos*, 806 F.2d 344 (2d Cir. 1986), cert. *denied*, 481 US 1048 (1987), which held that a preliminary injunction was proper in order to prevent defendant from making a judgment uncollectible.

[161] P.L. 101-647, § 2501(a).

[162] References in the text to "federal bankruptcy laws" and to the "Bankruptcy Code" mean and refer to the Bankruptcy Code of 1978, as amended, 11 USC §§ 101 *et seq.*

[163] 11 U.S.C. § 541.

[164] 11 U.S.C. § 548.

[165] 11 U.S.C. § 522(b). Florida, for example, denies the availability of the federal exemptions, except those set forth in 11 U.S.C. § 522(d)(10), to its residents. Fla. Stat. §§ 222.20, 222.201 (1991).

[166] 11 U.S.C. § 101(29).

[167] 11 U.S.C. § 727(a).

[168] HR Rep. No. 595, 95th Cong., 1st Sess. 384 (1977).

[169] *See, e.g., McCormick v. Security State Bank*, 822 F.2d 806 (8th Cir. 1987); *In Re Schmit*, 71 B.R. 587 (D.Minn. 1987); *In Re Tveten*, 70 B.R. 529 (D. Minn. 1987).

[170] HR Rep. No. 595, 95th Cong., 1st Sess. 361 (1977); S. Rep. No. 989, 95th Cong., 2d Sess. 76 (1978). *See also In Re Johnson*, 80 B.R. 953 (D. Minn. 1987).

[171] On the state level, Florida has recently enacted Fla. Stat. § 222.30 (1991), effective October 1, 1993, which provides that a conversion of nonexempt assets into exempt assets with the intent to hinder, delay, or defraud a creditor may be set aside. The provision may have been enacted to counter the argument that where a debtor converts his nonexempt bank account into an exempt annuity, that no "transfer" has taken place, and the UFTA is not applicable.

[172] 18 USC §§ 1956, 1957.

[173] PL 99-570, Title XIII, § 1352 (a).

[174] The term "specified unlawful activity" is defined in § 1956(b)(7) as follows:

> (7) the term "specified unlawful activity" means—
> (A) any act or activity constituting an offense listed in section 1961(1) of this title except an act which is indictable under subchapter II of chapter 53 of title 31;
> (B) with respect to a financial transaction occurring in whole or in part in the United States, an offense against a foreign nation involving—
> (i) the manufacture, importation, sale, or distribution of a controlled substance (as such term is defined for the purposes of the Controlled Substances Act);

Endnotes

(ii) kidnapping, robbery, or extortion; or

(iii) fraud, or any scheme or attempt to defraud, by or against a foreign bank (as defined in paragraph 7 of section 1(b) of the International Banking Act of 1978;

(C) any act or acts constituting a continuing criminal enterprise, as that term is defined in section 408 of the Controlled Substances Act (21 USC, 848);

(D) an offense under section 152 (relating to concealment of assets; false oaths and claims; bribery), section 215 (relating to commissions or gifts for procuring loans), any of sections 500 through 503 (relating to certain counterfeiting offenses), section 513 (relating to securities of states and private entities), section 542 (relating to entry of goods by means of false statements), section 545 (relating to smuggling goods into the United States), section 549 (relating to removing goods from Customs custody), section 641 (relating to public money, property, or records), section 656 (relating to theft, embezzlement, or misapplication by bank officer or employee), section 657 (relating to lending, credit, and insurance institutions), section 658 (relating to property mortgaged or pledged to farm credit agencies), section 666 (relating to theft or bribery concerning programs receiving federal funds), section 793, 794, or 798 (relating to espionage), section 875 (relating to interstate communications), section 1005 (relating to fraudulent bank entries), 1006 (relating to fraudulent federal credit institution entries), 1007 (relating to fraudulent Federal Deposit Insurance transactions), 1014 (relating to fraudulent loan or credit applications), 1032 (relating to concealment of assets from conservator, receiver, or liquidating agent of financial institution), section 1201 (relating to kidnapping), section 1203 (relating to hostage taking), section 1708 (theft from the mail), section 2113 or 2114 (relating to bank and postal robbery and theft), or section 2319 (relating to copyright infringement) of this title, a felony violation of the Chemical Diversion and Trafficking Act of 1988 (relating to precursor and essential chemicals), section 590 of the Tariff Act of 1930 (19 U.S.C. 1590) (relating to aviation smuggling), section 422 of the Controlled Substances Act (relating to transportation of drug paraphernalia), section 38(c) (relating to criminal violations) of the Arms Export Control Act, section 11 (relating to violations) of the Export Administration Act of 1979, section 206 (relating to penalties) of the International Emergency Economic Powers Act, section 16 (relating to offenses and punishment) of the Trading with the Enemy Act, any felony violation of section 9(c) of the Food Stamp Act of 1977 (relating to food stamp fraud) involving a quantity of coupons having a value of not less than $5,000, or any felony violation of the Foreign Corrupt Practices Act), or

(E) a felony violation of the Federal Water Pollution Control Act (33 U.S.C. 1251 et seq.), the Ocean Dumping Act (33 U.S.C. 1401 *et seq.*), the Act to Prevent Pollution from Ships (33 U.S.C. 1901 *et seq.*), the Safe Drinking Water Act (42 U.S.C. 300f *et seq.*), or the Resources Conservation and Recovery Act (42 U.S.C. § 6901 *et seq.*)."

[175] Fines of up to $500,000 or twice the value of the property involved in the transaction, whichever is greater, or up to twenty years in prison, or both.

[176] Fines up to the greater of $10,000 or the value of the property involved.

[177] An intentional and knowing disregard of the nature of the funds involved.

[178] *E.g.*, New Jersey.

[179] *See, e.g.*, Kentucky R.S. § 427.060—$5,000 homestead exemption.

[180] *See., e.g.*, Fla. Const., Art. X, § 4, which provides a homestead exemption, unlimited in value, for up to 160 acres if located outside of a municipality, and up to half an acre if located inside of a municipality.

[181] Typically, an otherwise exempt homestead will be available to satisfy purchase money obligations, home improvement mechanics liens, and tax obligations.

[182] Id.

[183] Arkansas requires a person to be married or the head of a family. Ark. Const. Art. 9, § 3.

[184] In common law and statutory law, a life estate is the ownership of land for the duration of a person's life. The owner of a life estate is called a "life tenant." Although the ownership of a life estate is of limited duration because it ends at the death of the person who is the "measuring life," the life tenant has the right to enjoy the

benefits of ownership of the property, including income derived from rent or other uses of the property, during his or her possession.

[185] Alternative structuring, depending upon the facts and circumstances, may involve the life tenant providing all of the consideration and gifting the remainder.

[186] 26 U.S.C. § 2702.

[187] Treas. Reg. § 25.2702-5(a).

[188] *In Re Reed*, 700 F.2d 986 (5th Cir. 1983), where an "eve of bankruptcy payoff of a homestead encumbrance prevented debtor's bankruptcy discharge; *See also In Re Sayler*, 68 B.R. 111 (D. Kan. 1986); *Michelson v. Anderson* 31 B.R. 635 (D. Minn. 1982).

[189] 15 U.S.C. §§ 1671–1677.

[100] 15 U.S.C. § 1673(a). Garnishment cannot exceed the lesser of 25 percent of after tax earnings, or the amount by which such earnings exceed thirty times the federal minimum hourly wage. *See* § 1673(b) for exceptions to § 1673(a).

[191] *Dunlop v. First National Bank of Arizona*, 399 F. Supp. 855 (D.C. Ariz. 1975); *Usery v. First National Bank of Arizona*, 586 F.2d 107 (9th Cir. 1978).

[192] *John O. Melby & Co. Bank v. Anderson*, 276 N.W.2d 274 (Wis. 1979).

[193] 15 U.S.C. § 1673(b); *see, e.g.,* Kan. Stat. § 60-2310.

[194] Fla. Stat. § 222.11 (effective 10/1/93). Prior Florida law did not impose a time limitation. Disposable earnings of a head of a family in excess of $500 per week may be garnished if agreed to in writing by the debtor. *See also* Minn. Stat. § 550.37, subd. 13.

[195] Fla. Stat. § 222.11(2)(c) (2013).

[196] *See, e.g., In Re Schlein,* 114 B.R. 780 (M.D. Fla. 1990); *Matter of Glickman,* 126 B.R. 124 (M.D. Fla. 1991).

[197] *See, e.g.,* Ala. Stat. § 16-25-23; Fla. Stat. § 222.14; Neb. Stat. § 44-371(1) (limited to $10,000); Ohio Stat. § 3911.10; N.J. Stat. 17B:24–7(a).

[198] 88 B.R. 436 (S.D. Fla. 1988).

[199] Fla. Stat. § 222.14 (2013).

[200] 986 F.2d 436 (11th Cir. 1993).

[201] 612 So.2d 572 (Fla. 1993).

[202] *Cf., In Re Pizzi,* 153 B.R. 357 (S.D. Fla. 1993).

[203] A plan that is subject to Title I of ERISA, PL 93-406.

[204] 112 S.Ct. 2242 (1992).

[205] *See Present Law and Issues Relating to the Treatment of Qualified Pension Plans in Personal Bankruptcy*, JCS-16-91, 102nd Cong., 1st Sess. (11/27/91), for an excellent description of the pre-Patterson confusion.

[206] 112 S.Ct. at 2246.

[207] Id.

[208] 148 B.R. 930 (C.D. Cal. 1992). *See also In Re Hall*, 151 B.R. 412 (W.D. Mich. 1993).

[209] 29 C.F.R. § 2510.3-3(b), (c)(1) (1988).

[210] 149 B.R. 760 (E.D. N.Y. 1993).

[211] § 416(c)(2)(A). Keogh plans covering only partners and sole proprietors are not "ERISA" plans.

[212] Many states have statutes exempting a debtor's interest in a qualified retirement plan from creditors' claims. *See, e.g.*, NY Debt. & Cred. Law § 282(2)(e); Fla. Stat. § 222.21; Tex. Prop. Code § 42.0021(a).

[213] *See, e.g.*, Tex. Prop. Code § 42.0021(a); 31 Okla. Stat. § 1; Wis. Stat. § 815.18; Fla. Stat. § 222.21.

[214] *See, e.g., Ameritrust Co. v. Derakhshan*, #92 CV0931 (N.D. Ohio 7/16/93).

Endnotes

[215] *See, e.g.,* Colo. Rev. Stat. § 13-54-102(1); Fla. Stat. § 222.13; Ill. Stat. Ch. 73, par. 850; Ind. Code § 27-1-12-14; Iowa Code § 511.37; Kan. Stat. § 40-414; Mich. Stat. § 24.12207; Minn. Stat. § 550.37; Ohio Rev. Code § 3911.10; Tex. Ins. Code Art. 21.22; Wis. Stat. § 815.18(19).

[216] Ill. Stat. Ch.73, par. 850 (proceeds payable to spouse, child, or other dependent of insured); Ind. Code § 12-1-12-14 (spouse, children, dependent relative, or creditor); Ohio Rev. Code § 3911.10 (spouse, children, dependent relative, creditor, or trustee of any of the foregoing).

[217] *See, e.g.,* Ariz. Rev. Stat. § 20-1131; Cal. C.C.P. § 699.720(a)(6); Fla. Stat. §

[218] For both asset protection and estate tax savings purposes.

[219] *See* Rosen, "Foreign Irrevocable Life Insurance Trusts Can Save Estate and Income Tax," 10 *J. Tax of Investments* 23 (Autumn 1992), for a discussion of interesting tax planning possibilities in connection with an offshore life insurance trust.

[220] New Zealand may act on behalf of the Cook Islands in foreign affairs and defense issues, but only when requested to do so by the Cook Islands government and with its advice and consent.

[221] International Trusts Act 1984, as amended.

[222] Id., § 13B.

[223] Id., § 13F.

[224] Id., § 13C.

[225] Id., § 13G.

[226] Id., § 13D.

[227] Id., § 13J.

[228] Id., § 13A.

[229] The Hague Convention on the Law Applicable to Trusts and on Their Recognition (Oct. 20, 1984) (hereinafter, the "Convention"). Although § 4(2) of The Trusts (Foreign Elements) Law 1987 contains an excellent choice of governing law provision.

[230] Fraudulent Dispositions Law, 1989, § 4(3).

[231] Id., § 6.

[232] Bankruptcy Law (Revised) §§ 107–109.

[233] Confidential Relationships (Preservation) Law, 1976.

[234] A settlor is "insolvent" under the law if his or her liabilities (actual, contingent or prospective) exceed the value of his or her assets. No creditor's claim is considered contingent or prospective unless the settlor had actual notice of the claim or of facts and circumstances

which would render him/her liable to such a claim. § 42A(3)(b). *See also* Bankruptcy (Register of Dispositions) Regulations 1990.

[235] Also known as the Isle of Mona.

[236] Trusts Act 1992 § 64.

[237] Id., § 6.

[238] Id., § 12(4).

[239] Id., § 16.

[240] Id., § 4.

[241] Id., § 7(6).

[242] Id., § 7(7). *See* Law of Property Act § 149; Bankruptcy Act § 42 and Reciprocal Enforcement of Judgments Act [Cap 135].

[243] Trusts Ordinance 1990 § 4.

[244] Id., § 14.

[245] Id., § 61(1). Subsection 2 places the burden of proving the settlor's insolvency on the creditor asserting that fact. Insolvency is defined in § 2(1) as "being subject to liabilities, whether actual, contingent, or prospective, of which the value exceeds that of the assets available to meet such liabilities as they become due…"

246 The Foreign Account Tax Compliance Act, enacted in March 2010, under which US individual taxpayers must report information about certain foreign financial accounts and offshore assets on Form 8938 and attach it to their income tax return, if the total asset value exceeds the appropriate reporting threshold. In addition, to avoid being withheld upon, a foreign financial institution may register with the IRS, obtain a Global Intermediary Identification Number (GIIN) and report certain information on US accounts to the IRS. See Section IX C 2, below.

247 Glasson, *International Trust Laws*, A17.25 (1992).

248 See article from *Philadelphia Inquirer* online at: http://articles.philly.com/1993-10-02/news/25937578_1_forest-fire-motor-home-howards

249 *US v. Northeastern Pharmaceutical and Chemical Company, Inc.*, 579 F.Supp. 823 (W.D.Mo. 1984), *aff'd in part and rev'd in part*, 810 F.2d 726 (8th Cir. 1986).

250 42 U.S.C. § 9601, *et seq.* Other federal environmental liability statutes include: the Resource Conservation and Recovery Act, 42 U.S.C. § 6901, *et. seq*; the Federal Water Pollution Control Act, 33 U.S.C. § 1251, *et. seq*; the Clean Air Act, 42 U.S.C. § 7401, *et seq.*; the Toxic Substances Control Act, 15 U.S.C. § 2601, *et seq.*; and the Emergency Planning and Community Right to Know Act of 1986, 42 U.S.C. § 11001, *et seq.*

251 *See, e.g., City of North Miami, Florida v. Berger*, 828 F.Supp. 401 (E.D. Va. 1993).

Endnotes

[252] *See, e.g., City of Phoenix, Arizona v. Garbage Services Company*, 827 F.Supp. 600 (D.Ariz. 1993); *but see*, 40 C.F.R. Part 300 (April 29, 1992), where, in the preamble, the EPA said:

[253] Not a reported case, but much publicized. *See, e.g.*, Curtis, *Old Knights and New Champions: Kaye, Scholer, The Office of Thrift Supervision, and the Pursuit of the Dollar*, 66 S. Cal. L. Rev. 985 (March, 1993).

[254] 29 U.S.C. § 1109(a).

[255] 29 U.S.C. § 1002(21)(A).

[256] *See, e.g., Rosenberg v. Aarnel Funding Corp.*, 575 So.2d 753 (Fla 3rd Dist. 1991).

[257] Even though no penalty is imposed for failure to report an incomplete gift, the authors strongly recommend compliance with the regulation, as a means of documenting the planning, if for no other reason.

[258] Treas. Reg. § 25.2511-2(j).

[259] Treas. Reg. § 1.6031-1(a)(1).

[260] 26 U.S.C. §§ 671-679.

[261] Treas. Reg. § 1.671-4(a).

[262] 26 U.S.C. § 671.

[263] 26 U.S.C. §§ 671–679.

[264] IRS instructions for Form 3520, page 2.

[265] IRS instructions for Form 3520, page 1.

[266] 26 USC § 6048(b).

[267] 1997-1 C.B. 6.

[268] *Burnet v. Logan*, 283 US 404 (1931).

[269] Id.

[270] AV Preeminent® is a certification mark of Reed Elsevier Properties Inc.

www.ingramcontent.com/pod-product-compliance
Lightning Source LLC
Chambersburg PA
CBHW071428170526
45165CB00001B/443